MANAGEMENT STRATEGIES FOR
THE
CLOUD
REVOLUTION

(((**MANAGEMENT STRATEGIES FOR**)))

THE
CLOUD
REVOLUTION

How Cloud Computing Is
Transforming Business and Why 004.36
You Can't Afford to Be Left Behind B114

(((**CHARLES BABCOCK**)))

New York   Chicago   San Francisco
Lisbon   London   Madrid   Mexico City   Milan
New Delhi   San Juan   Seoul   Singapore
Sydney   Toronto

The *McGraw·Hill* Companies

Copyright © 2010 by Charles Babcock. All rights reserved. Printed in the United States of America. Except as permitted under the United States Copyright Act of 1976, no part of this publication may be reproduced or distributed in any form or by any means, or stored in a data base or retrieval system, without the prior written permission of the publisher.

1 2 3 4 5 6 7 8 9 0   DOC/DOC   1 5 4 3 2 1 0

ISBN: 978-0-07-174075-3
MHID: 0-07-174075-9

Design by Lee Fukui and Mauna Eichner

McGraw-Hill books are available at special quantity discounts to use as premiums and sales promotions, or for use in corporate training programs. To contact a representative please visit the Contact Us pages at www.mhprofessional.com.

I dedicate this book to my wife,

Kathleen Linda Curtis,

who is my first mate on

the good sloop *Calypso Poet,*

my first reviewer in all endeavors, and

the star in the Bahá'í sky by which I steer.

CONTENTS

ACKNOWLEDGMENTS

To all the outstanding people in the Silicon Valley and elsewhere who have tried to educate me through e-mail, phone interviews, numerous face-to-face sit-down sessions, and the occasional beer at the Thirsty Bear or 21st Amendment, I owe an everlasting debt of thanks.

They include Amit Pandey, CEO of Terracotta, who illustrated what in-memory software could do versus disk-store systems; early Linux advocate Mark Towfiq, who co-led the modernization of e-commerce at Walmart.com alongside Ari Zilka, currently Terracotta's CTO; Bogomil Balkansky at VMware for explaining key elements of virtualization; Winston Bumpus, president of the Distributed Management Task Force (and chief of standards at VMware); Simon Crosby, CTO at the XenSource unit of Citrix Systems, also for highlighting key elements of virtualization; Margaret Lewis, at AMD, for a cross-vendor point of view on industry trends; the open source leader Rod Johnson, former CEO of SpringSource, now part of VMware, for illustrating how open source works, along with Brian Behlendorf, an original member of the Apache Web server project; Sanjiva Weerawarana, CEO at WSO2, for his understanding of lightweight Web services; and Executive Vice President Paul Cormier at Red Hat for his perspective on early Web search operations. And thanks also to Marty Goetz, president of the former Applied Data Research, who ushered a newcomer into the complexities of large system software and who, many years ago, was instrumental in starting software's march as a force independent of any particular brand of hardware.

Much of the thinking in this book found its first expression in truncated form in the United Business Media publication *InformationWeek,* my current employer. Two editors there assisted me in direct and indirect ways to make this book possible. One is Art Wittmann, now editor of *InformationWeek* Analytics and a steadying voice in the debate over the direction of IT, the network, and the cloud; the second is Chris Murphy, an editor with rare skill at working with the strengths (and weaknesses) of writers. Thanks also to Government CIO and Plug into the Cloud Editor John Foley at Information-Week.com, who helped guide the process that led to this book's creation, and Editor in Chief Rob Preston, who in a period of constrained resources still gave the go-ahead and offered encouragement and advice.

As much as I am indebted to them, it is still correct to say that any mistakes in this work are purely my own and no one else is accountable.

INTRODUCTION

There's a kind of awe associated with what's called "cloud computing," an impression that something momentous is afoot, as if the man behind the curtain was about to unveil something really big—and this time, for real.

I think it's those big data centers that we keep hearing about, the ones that Google, Yahoo!, Microsoft, Amazon, Sales force.com, and Facebook have been building. In Chicago, Microsoft threw open the doors to its newest data center in September, and a truck backed in over the concrete floor, depositing a container filled with racks of servers. Instead of being unloaded, the container was plugged in, and more than 2,000 servers instantly came to life. There were 11 similar containers already in operation and room for 44 more, while on the second story of the building, hardware in a more traditional, raised-floor data center was already humming away.

Microsoft's facility is designed for 300,000 servers, and according to Microsoft's president of servers and tools, Bob Muglia, as best he knows, it's the largest data center on earth.

A short while before Microsoft opened its doors, Google had opened a window on what had previously been the secret design of its own data centers. A Google camera crew showed an unpretentious-looking technician, possibly a recent high school graduate, mounting a razor scooter and scooting along the warehouse floor to a server unit. He extracted a failed server from the rack and inserted a new server, a unit that appeared to be about 3.5 inches thick, with a sheet metal baffle to keep the heat-generating parts separate from the cooler parts of the machine. That's not how they do it in the enterprise data center. This is not your father's data center.

Google and Amazon.com pioneered these concepts, and Microsoft and others have picked them up and produced their own implementations. When data centers such as this are built out of what are basically PC parts, with one server cluster consisting of thousands of servers, when very-large-scale parallel processing software is applied to the cluster, and when the governing software routes jobs around hardware failures, you have something new, a "cloud" data center. It is a string of 12 or more such data centers around the world that powers the marvelous Google search engine. And more are being built next to 2 cents per kilowatt hour sources of hydroelectric energy rather than the 11 cents per kilowatt hour energy that powers the computers on which this book was edited. Energy makes up a quarter of the expense of running a data center; cloud data centers take advantage of low-cost energy sites. The enterprise data center, with its need to be close to headquarters or manufacturing, can't do that.

Granted, some claim that "the cloud" is just another cycle in our seemingly endless series of technology enthusiasms, only to be followed by disappointment. Gartner says that "the cloud" is at the peak of its "hype" cycle, where the highest hopes are invested in it, and at the same time, it's at the top of the list of innovations likely to be adopted in the coming year. That in itself is a rare convergence.

The last hype cycle brought us the dot-com boom, followed by an even more dramatic bust. That boom reflected a fever for Web traffic and led to investment in sites meant to attract a million visitors a week, with imaginary profits to follow. The cloud is more real than the dot-com boom.

The cloud is a set of major productivity gains in computing, each of which is a multiplier of standard computer power in its own right. These multipliers are converging in this new style of data center, combined with a new empowerment of the end user. We are close to moving beyond the world of known computing patterns into a field of dreams, where such data centers are built partly in the belief that end users will not be able to resist their raw compute power or the powerful services that will be created there. I believe that at some point, these data centers will be linked together, backing each other up over the Internet until the old Sun Microsystems dictum, "the network is the computer," finally comes true. This self-reinforcing grid of computer power will reach out to end users in all sorts of unforeseen ways, finally becoming an all-enveloping embrace.

Have you been bumped into recently by someone walking down the street who is so absorbed in his iPhone or some other electronic device that he can't be bothered to notice the traffic around him? Well, it's going to get a lot worse. The range and depth of digital services that will flow out of the cloud will be more engaging than those currently available. Within a year, even the most detached observer will say that a fundamental shift is underway, with the human culture that's captured on the display of a small digital device being primary and other influences, such as education, literature, fine arts, and film, being secondary. Even skeptics will concede, most of them disapprovingly, that a revolution of historic proportions is taking place.

It will be hard to know how to position your company in the face of this inexorable, omnipresent shift to a more intense digital culture. But with an understanding of what the cloud is all about and how it's likely to evolve, it will be possible to form a strategy for survival and advancement in the coming era.

As we shall explore in this book, at its heart, the cloud is a shift in how end users will do the bulk of their computing. It's assumed at this early stage that "services that previously resided in the client, including e-mail, photo and video storage and office applications" will move off the PC device and into the cloud, according to a paper by Google's leading data center engineers. One needs only to look to MySpace, flickr, YouTube, and Facebook to see that such a shift is already underway.

But a more serious part of their computing, the way they conduct business, which was formerly done on their Black-Berry, netbook, laptop, or PC, will also move into the cloud. New layers of computing will be added to old patterns. Even as the data centers on the Internet get larger, the devices on which end users do their direct computing are likely to shrink, two contrary trends that must be reconciled if you're going to end up in the right position to be part of the cloud revolution.

But to the business strategist, the cloud means a good deal more than that. There will be a shift toward being able to rely on large clusters of servers on the Internet for either steady-state operations or the occasional needed surges of compute power—at prices below the cost of running the corporate data center. Businesses large and small will have the power to do things that they couldn't do before, do them faster, and reach customers more effectively when they make the right moves.

A new platform has emerged with which to engage customers and provide universal access to the business. Many new possibilities for interacting with prospects and engaging with customers are taking shape. The people you will be capable of reaching tomorrow wouldn't have dreamed of walking through your doors today.

If anything, business is going to find it harder to sell to well-informed consumers, who roam about the Internet at will as if they owned the world. The cloud has many potentially unpleasant connotations for traditional businesses—instant, acidic reviews by the most superficially disgruntled consumers, sharing their upset with millions. At the same time, it's going to offer new opportunities to relate to customers and understand why they came to you in the first place—and what they may want next.

In its most popular form, such as Amazon's Elastic Cloud Compute (EC2), cloud computing is a reorganization of external resources into a hitherto hard to conceive of set of computing services. Computing cycles of nearly any magnitude can be tapped at will. The amount of resources devoted to the job expands if, say, a surge in customer traffic makes it advisable to do so. And this expansive data center accessed through the Internet can be utilized at low hourly rates with the swipe of a credit card.

Perhaps the single most compelling feature of the cloud is that it is programmatically accessible by outsiders, the end users who have work for all those concentrated processing units. Automated processes have been built in to make cloud services readily available to anyone, regardless of location, as long as that person can pay the hourly rate. It's something like iTunes. You upload a small set of information related to yourself and get back a favorite song, without having to appear at a store and sort through bins. However, in the cloud, it's an enterprise application that goes out over the wire and the results of processing all that data come back.

No single technology is responsible for the advent of the cloud. Broadband communications, Web standards, multicore servers, and the ability to manage large groups of computers as if they were a single machine—these are the components of cloud computing. Mix them together, along with a tendency to organize business applications as services, and things will never be the same again. This new computing power will change the way companies will do business.

Today, cloud computing is most frequently thought of as an external resource, the public cloud. Tomorrow, you will find your organization reorganizing its data center around cloud principles. If this is done adroitly, your internal cloud will be smaller and less expensive than the former data center. That's because for years corporate data centers have been over-built. Now they will be right-sized and will align easily with an external cloud that can absorb the spikes that you send it. You will be provisioning your own facilities for near steady-state operation, rather than workload peaks. When unusual demands occur, say, in accounting at the end of the quarter or in the holiday rush at the end of the year, you will be able to move them off to the external cloud. You'll have to pay for the time you use, but immense savings will be gained by avoiding that former compulsive overprovisioning.

This hybrid cloud, a mix of external public resources and reorganized internal resources, and how it will affect what your company can do are what this book is about. No such hybrid clouds have been designed from the ground up yet—it's too early—but they're evolving out of today's infrastructure. In effect, your data center of the future is a hybrid cloud.

Cloud computing will solve the problem of overprovisioning and the tendency of data center budgets to invest heavily in keeping the lights on and the computers running, when what they really should be doing is solving new problems. The cloud will also bring its own complexities and management challenges, and some of them will prove worthy successors to the challenges of the past.

But most of all, the cloud will bring a new way of doing things and a whole new set of opportunities. *Management Strategies for the Cloud Revolution* is about this break from the shackles of the past and the competitive landscape that is likely to emerge as a result.

THE CLOUD REVOLUTION

In works of art, from the photos of Ansel Adams to the paintings of ancient Chinese artists, clouds have often been given tangible form and purpose. In Adams's arid West, they served as a backdrop to granite peaks, holding out the promise of rain. To the Chinese, an all-encompassing mist allows special features to emerge out of the mountain landscape, or sometimes there will be a series of ridges as far as the eye can see, their bases cloaked in clouds—an illusion of infinity.

For many years the cloud has played a more prosaic role among the squares, rectangles, and circles of the architecture diagrams of technology projects, but its meaning has been ambiguous. "The cloud" was a euphemism for everything that was beyond the data center or out on the network. The action that affected the project at hand was in the data center; the cloud was a mishmash of remotely connected parts and network protocols that didn't have much to do with the immediate problem. No matter how nonartistic the systems architect, he could always represent the cloud—an offhand, squiggly circle in the background of his scheme.

As business use of the Internet has grown, the cloud has moved from a throwaway symbol in the architect's diagram to something more substantial and specific: it has become the auxiliary computing, supplied through Web site applications and Web services, such as credit checks and customer address lookups, that backed up the operation of standard business applications in the enterprise data center. Businesses built around Web services, such as Google, Amazon.com, and eBay, produced a new type of data center that was more standardized, more automated, and built from mass-produced personal computer parts. Access to these data centers was kept under wraps for several years as their builders sought to maintain a competitive advantage. As the notion caught on that it was possible to provide more and more powerful services over the Internet, cloud computing came to mean an interaction between an end user, whether a consumer or a business computing specialist, and one of these services "in the cloud."

When Microsoft appeared on the scene determined to stake a larger claim to this new form of computing, it started talking about its facilities in Chicago and Ireland as a new type of data center. Google, which played a key role in establishing the type, began illustrating key features of its data centers, and by late 2008 it was clear that the term *cloud* meant not only making use of innovative computing services out on the Internet, but sometimes gaining access through the Internet to computers in a powerful new type of data center with large resources available. Part of the appeal of using this type of data center was that you could pay for only what you used. The cloud had moved front and center in thinking about the next wave of computing. The resource might still be described as being located in a squiggly circle, but oh, what a resource. The cloud deals with customers on a broad scale and with a level of sophisticated automation never seen before. The vague goings-on out there in the cloud had taken on more significance and heft.

Even so, it is still difficult to summarize in a nutshell for the CEO, COO, and CFO what your company might do with cloud computing. Those who have watched the progression just described sense that something big is under way, but it's hard to explain what it's all about with a sound bite. Rather, there is a large-scale experiment under way on many fronts to determine what might be done "in the cloud."

Many people agree that cloud computing is the next phase of business and personal computing, but why call it "cloud"? The term is ambiguous or, worse, amorphous. For 25 years, during tours of duty at *Computerworld, Digital News, Interactive Week,* and *InformationWeek,* I've watched visitors draw the cloud in whiteboard diagrams. It was the discard part of the picture. But first, what exactly is the cloud, and how did it go from something that you could ignore to something that we can't seem to stop talking about?

Defining the Cloud

There are many definitions of the cloud—too many for any one to have achieved a rigorous meaning. It's most specifically described as software as a service, where a software application can be accessed online, as in Salesforce.com, Google Apps, or Zoho. It also takes the form of infrastructure as a service, where a user goes to a site such as Amazon Web Services' Elastic Compute Cloud (EC2) and rents time on a server. It also takes the form of platform as a service, where certain tools are made available with which to build software to run in the host cloud. These descriptors are common currency in technology circles and have been defined by a government agency, the National Institute of Standards and Technology. They have currency, but I don't put much stock in them. I think they are temporary snapshots of a rapidly shifting formation.

Nevertheless, the marketers have heard the buzz, and suddenly they want to describe what they're doing as part of the cloud. "Cloud Computing: Real Approach or Buzzword Bingo?" asked the headline in an electronic newsletter crossing my screen recently.

So it's possible today that when the CEO asks his technical staff what's all this he's hearing about the cloud, the IT directors and Web site managers will start describing its parts, then argue over what's required in the cloud, disagreeing immediately and sometimes vigorously. The corporate IT staff knows the cloud when it sees it; it just can't tell you what it is.

The CEO has heard that the cloud is "the next phase of Internet computing," but what that means is now more muddled than ever. He shakes his head as he walks away. If the members of his staff are arguing about what it is, chances are that they're not going to be able to tell him the thing he most wants to know: how's it going to affect him and the business.

Lately he's heard that it's what consumers are doing as they increasingly use smart handheld devices to download products such as iTunes. With seeming whimsy, these consumers turn some companies into huge winners, while bypassing others. So a subsidiary meaning of "cloud" is the next phase of business computing. For such a thing to be true, more of each business will have to move out onto the Internet. Much of this book will discuss that prospect and what form the next phase of business computing and business in the cloud age is most likely to take.

But to answer the CEO's question more directly, let's try to say what the cloud is. In late 2009, I saw Andi Gutmans, CEO of Zend Technologies, address a gathering of 500 PHP developers in San Jose, where he said, "I'm not going to try to tell you what cloud is. Everyone's got their own definition."

Gutmans is coauthor of the modern version of PHP, which has become the most popular language on the Internet; in its 5.3 release, PHP is undoubtedly the leading language with which to build cloud applications. If Gutmans can't say what cloud is, I'm not altogether sure anyone else should try, but we must still forge ahead.

Many people point to Travelocity's airline reservation system and Apple's iTunes Store as examples of cloud computing. While both of these are sophisticated e-commerce systems running on big Internet data centers, they are not what I would call cloud computing.

With the iTunes example, the so-called cloud is basically controlling the end user consumer, taking the few digital bits of information on song selection and credit card data that the user inputs and returning a song as a larger collection of bits. It has one purpose, and it executes the same electronic transaction for each end user, although shoppers can certainly pick out the specific tune they want. Many iTunes enthusiasts believe that "the cloud" is working for them. At 99 cents per digital transfer, I think they're working for a tiny subsection of cloud real estate owned by Apple.

To some extent, the same can be said for eBay and Amazon.com's retail store, although admittedly each keeps making use of more and more bits from the end user to supply more services than a simple digital media download. They clearly deserve citizenship in the emerging cloud nation and are representative of its pioneers.

Google comes closer yet to a solid definition of the cloud, with its massive data centers around the world powering instant responses to millions of users. At Google headquarters in Mountain View, California, there's a display of a revolving world, with graphic spikes rising above population centers like Tokyo, Hong Kong, and Singapore. The spikes are a visualization of search engine use by location, showing that hundreds of thousands of searches are going on in each place simultaneously. The display is refreshed in real time; it's like a panorama of ongoing, intense human inquisitiveness around the globe.

Google's operations have many of the characteristics of the cloud: a modern data center resource, built from low-cost components, managed as a whole, activated by end users on the network, and delivering automated results without either party knowing much about the other's systems. This applies to both Google's search engine and what it calls its Google App Engine, where developers build applications to run in the Google cloud. But what distinguishes some data centers that are labeled as being "in the cloud," like Google's, from some others that meet this description without by common consent being included as well? In the end, even the description given here is inadequate to define where the essence of the cloud lies. Among good technologists, this definition would set off a debate that would still be going as the search visualization spikes descended over Los Angeles and began to rise above Honolulu, Tokyo, and Beijing.

Instead of debating the technology innovations in the cloud data centers—and there are many of them—we need to stand this debate on its head. It's not its most prominent feature, the huge Internet data center, that is the cloud's defining element. Rather, that is just one building block. The cloud is actually a number of advances—the data centers, the Web's setting of conventions for loosely coupled systems (two systems that don't know very much about each other), and an ability to activate virtualized servers remotely via standard Web services—that converge to give the cloud its enticing power.

It's an interesting convergence, but in fact it's impossible to talk about the cloud without citing how anyone can use it at low hourly rates. Those big data centers produce economies of scale that can be delivered to the end user, whether that user is an individual or a business. Amazon charges 8.5 cents per hour for the use of a server in its EC2 cloud infrastructure. Rackspace, another provider of cloud infrastructure (servers and storage, with automated self provisioning), has lowered the cost further to 1.5 cents an hour, although at such rates it may be bidding for market share, not making profits. These rates are presumed to be lower than corporate data center costs of operation because fewer staff members manage many more servers through automated controls. Microsoft executives in statements to the Chicago press said they will manage their new data center there with 45 people, including the janitors and security guards. It's a data center designed for 300,000 servers, although it hadn't reached that number as this was being written. Many corporate data centers have one system administrator focused on one application, or a handful of applications. In the cloud, one system administrator supervises hardware running hundreds of applications.

Beyond businesses, many consumer end users have shown an appetite for consuming new services on the Web. They enter personal data in MySpace; post pictures at flickr.com and both pictures and current commentaries in Facebook, and disclose professional associations on LinkedIn. The cloud offers a business model where many services, including massive amounts of computer server power, storage, and network bandwidth, can be made available at a low price, even a price that seems only slightly more expensive than free. The technology convergence has found expression in a new distribution model for computing. So in addition to technology, the cloud is a business model that makes a new form of computing widely available at prices that heretofore would have been considered impossible.

To the technology and business model, we must add one final defining characteristic. What people call "the cloud" today is activated by a few preset end user actions, such as telling Facebook to upload a picture or post a comment on a wall. In the deeper example of sending a workload to the cloud and telling it how it's to be run, the user has assumed a new relationship with the data center that has not been possible for most remote users in the past. The cloud gives the user "programmatic control" over a part of the data center, the ability to command a server in the data center to run the program she has selected and sent.

The cloud user doesn't have to ask someone to intervene to set up connections, turn on a powerful machine, and let him know what software is there to run. On the contrary, he "self-provisions" the computers he needs by swiping a credit card and clicking off a checklist of what servers he wants to activate with a mouse. For people who have a large task that they want to execute but don't want to make out a purchase order to buy a new server, await delivery, then ask IT staffers to configure it, this is as close to manna from heaven as they're going to get.

Despite the ambiguity of the definition of the cloud, a fundamental shift is under way. The data centers that serve the cloud seem to mesmerize those who have learned the details of one or gotten near one, and in truth, many end user services currently found in the applications on the desktop are likely to be served from the cloud in the future. These data centers are often large warehouse-style buildings, with few windows, surrounded by chain-link fences. Inside, row upon row of pizza box–style servers, or even smaller "blade" servers, are stuffed into racks standing seven feet tall. Amid the whir of fans and the hum of water pumps, row upon row of racks stretch into the distance.

Six years ago, I remember a debate over whether, if Microsoft built a data center that held 28,000 servers, it would be larger than Google's, but that debate is ridiculously out of date. Let's put this in perspective. Google declines to disclose how many servers its search engine runs on, lest it set off such an arms race. As it is, Microsoft boasts that the data center that it opened in September 2009 in Chicago to support its Azure cloud, the largest of six data centers that it plans to operate, will have 300,000 servers. And we know that Yahoo! sorts and indexes the results of its Web crawls (the process of assimilating all the documents and information on the Web) and executes other information sorting on an internal cloud of 25,000 servers, and that doesn't include running its content Web sites or conducting searches.

Google acknowledged in June 2009 that one of its data centers held 45,000 servers. I am guessing that Google's total reaches 500,000 to 600,000 servers spread over at least 12 international data centers, and that may be too low. It has drawn up a plan that will allow it to manage a million or more servers.

The point is that few of the largest enterprise data centers claim 45,000 servers; some data centers in the cloud are being built on a scale never seen before. They tend to drive economies of scale that are not easy to duplicate anywhere else.

These data centers are frequently what people are referring to when they discuss the cloud. In common parlance, the cloud is all those servers out on the Internet that are delivering information and services to end users, wherever they may be. But such a description, in which we are still somewhat mesmerized by size, is not the point. In addition to assembling a lot of server power, the cloud does things differently than the way computing has been organized before. Big Internet data centers have existed since the advent of AltaVista, Lycos, Excite, and other early search engines.

One distinction is that these new data centers have been able to leave so many of the problems associated with traditional data centers behind. The traditional data center is labor-intensive and has many different kinds of servers, reflecting an evolution through several early models of computing supplied by different manufacturers. The cloud data centers are different. They seem to have been engineered at a stroke for a new set of priorities; all the servers are the same or closely related and are managed in the same way. They require fewer people. The traditional data center is overengineered and overinvested in hardware, trying to avoid machine failure. The cloud data center tolerates hardware failures and routes work around them. It solves through software the hardware problems that used to necessitate the shutdown of machines and replacement of parts. It ties together large numbers of low-cost parts and manages them as a single resource, and it performs accordingly. Thus, Amazon can tell you as soon as you make a purchase what other buyers like you also bought. And the marvelous Google search engine returns thousands of results from a multiple-keyword search in less than a second. Without the cloud, this speed wouldn't be possible.

But search and e-commerce are still child's play compared to what the cloud is capable of offering. Facebook, with at last count 326 million active users uploading text, photos, and video and manipulating content, comes a lot closer to showing the potential of the cloud, but it still falls short. Five years ago, such services would have seemed inconceivable. What will the new services look like five years from now?

From out of the cloud will come massive computing resources at prices that seem to defy economics—information and services that stream to the end user as if from some beneficent power. Like a river flowing from the mountains, the Internet "cloud" provides resources to distant points without incurring any extra charge. For example, you might get access to software that will help you design a sailboat to the latest principles of streamlined hull shapes. You might find advice and interactive guidance on how to cope with problems as you start a company. You might go through an interactive process, using video to show what your firm is doing, with venture capitalists who are looking for a worthy candidate in which to invest. Once you've tapped into the cloud, you cease to be an isolated individual and you become part of a larger digital cosmos, where everything is linked to everything.

These data centers on the network foster new kinds of software that in themselves are marvels of recent engineering. With the Hadoop cloud-based data engine, data is lifted off hundreds or thousands of disk drives in parallel without "thrashing" the drive spindles—that is, forcing the drive heads to move this way and that in the struggle to collect data from a spinning disk. Drive thrashing is how enterprise databases work, but it's much too time-consuming for the cloud. With Google Maps, an image of a particular place is offered on the screen before us, and as we move the cursor, the map extends in front of us as if it has no edge, no boundary. By following the cursor, we can travel as far as we wish. Somewhere in the Google data center, a sensor sees the direction of the cursor and anticipates the data that we'll need next, preloading it into the browser. In the cloud, the illusion of an endless resource somehow becomes a reality. Other systems can't do it, but the cloud can map to the ends of the earth.

The Shifting Boundary: Illusion versus Reality

So how much of the cloud is real and how much is illusion? It's the Internet that gives us a sense of connectedness and reach. That was true before the term *cloud computing* came to the fore. The Internet plus big data centers somehow still does not equal the cloud. What is it about the cloud that intrigues even otherwise worldly technologists? What is the breakthrough that everybody is talking about? That's what this book attempts to answer.

Critics Charge That the Cloud Isn't Real

Let's pause here for a second and concede that many computer industry leaders look at discussions of "cloud computing," perhaps including the one given here, and don't see
anything there. To them, it's all gaseous vapor. Hard-bitten,
skeptical technologists examine cloud discussions and see only
a set of technologies that they're familiar with and have understood for years. They don't consider them remarkable except
perhaps in scale, certainly not a breakthrough. They see a form
of plain vanilla Web services at work. What's the big deal?

These critics can be an antidote to boundless enthusiasm
about the cloud. Some enthusiasts have something old to sell,
but with "cloud" newly added to the product name. This adoption of the term by marketers has produced its own backlash.
Still, that doesn't explain why some discerning observers view
the term with a skepticism bordering on sarcasm.

Larry Ellison, CEO of Oracle, the commercial database
company, says that all the talk about cloud computing is a debate over style, not substance. The computing industry "is the
only industry that is more fashion driven than women's fashion," he said during an earnings call with Wall Street analysts
in the fall of 2008.

"Finally a tech exec willing to tell the truth about cloud
computing," applauded a respected writer on San Francisco's
online news network, CNet.

More recently, in a speech before the Churchill Club in
San Jose on September 22, 2009, Ellison elaborated: "All
'cloud' is is a computer attached to a network with databases,

operating systems, memory, microchips. All of a sudden it's 'the cloud.' What is the cloud? The cloud is water vapor. . . . Change 'cloud' to 'Internet' and give it back to these nitwits on Sand Hill Road."

Sand Hill Road is the road that slopes down the west side of Silicon Valley into Menlo Park, along which the venture capitalists have built their low-slung offices. I know people along that road; very few of them are nitwits. Some of them are busy at this moment giving millions of dollars to cloud computing start-ups.

For 25 years, Ellison has adroitly positioned his company at the head of various technology trends. He's slated to be paid $73 million this year, according to Bloomberg. Is cloud computing really going to become a major business trend if someone like Ellison treats it with a skepticism bordering on disdain?

Many would argue that defining the cloud in technology terms leads to a description that is less than the sum of its parts. Too many people are examining the details of the cloud to discover where the key advances occur. The cloud should be examined less through a microscope and more through the lens of business and technology convergence.

Think of small streams on a frozen mountainside. They all look familiar and insignificant until they are given a chance to converge in an ice field, which in turn starts a glacier moving down the valley. Boulders that had been immovable objects in the streams can now be pushed aside. The valley is about to be reshaped as the glacier expands and pushes against the landscape around it. But the cloud "glacier" will not be moving at the pace of its Ice Age predecessors; it's moving on Internet time, which compresses more motion into a day and a week than was previously conceivable over a much longer period. Soon this massive entity will be moving down the valley at a distinctly nonglacial pace; its progress will appear irresistible.

Each of the cloud's building blocks is a small stream in itself, but the force of their convergence is shaping up into something like that glacier. If you're a business computer user, reliant on an on-premises data center, there's no reason that you can't tap into the power of the cloud as well. If you're a small company that has only PCs and a small server or two, then the cloud can provide you with the power you need so that you don't have to build out a data center. Either way, it's wise to stay informed on developments in the cloud; at least don't turn a blind eye and get caught in its path.

But let's offer a more direct answer to Ellison's objections. For starters, the cloud is a continuation of the end user revolution that began with the MS-DOS PC in 1983–1984, and later with Windows and the Apple Macintosh. In focusing on the large data centers, most proponents of the cloud seem to think the amazing thing is the new power of the data center.

Soul of a New Machine:
Peer-to-Peer Computing

Think back to the PC Revolution, which unleashed a flood of computing horsepower to the desktop. PCs were soon linked to more powerful computers in individual businesses' self-contained data centers, but the PC's potential suffered in the process. The relationship was one of master to slave—data center server to PC—or, at best, master and servant. In many cases, the intelligence of the PC was discarded and the machine was reduced to the status of what's known in the industry as a dumb terminal, a device that couldn't think. It wasn't expected to think on its own, just follow orders. Its role was to display the results sent to it by the mainframe or other large server.

While the PC has continued to steadily gain in power, it had a second major weakness. Its design was focused on the individual, and that design helped to isolate it from the rest of the world. PC networks could be built to tie together fellow employees or the staffs of partner companies, but the PC couldn't get far in the outside world on its own on any kind of impulsive, ad hoc basis. It had to follow preset paths defined by larger systems and higher-ups in the organization.

The first phase of the Internet started to change that, giving the PC access to powerful servers on a worldwide network, servers that were eager to share information and content. But these gains to the user had come at a steep price. In many cases, participation on Tim Berners-Lee's World Wide Web meant that once again the PC had been reduced to a master/slave relationship. The early browser window might give end users access to the weather in Beijing or even the latest poetry in Prague, but after making a connection, all it could do was display the content sent to it by an Internet server. Every user was sent the same content. The first phase of Internet computing had taken a step backward, reducing the PC to a slave, a dumb terminal.

We're now in the second phase of the Internet, where browser windows occasionally show glimmers of intelligence. If you give it some bits, it gives you an airline ticket, an iTune, or a completed order for a bestseller from Amazon or B&N .com on a somewhat individualized basis. To accomplish that, the browser window is no longer a static device; small programs run in it, accomplishing work that the end user has directed, and those programs send instructions to the server and return responses. This is sometimes referred to as the second phase of Internet computing or Web 2.0, where the end user offers more inputs to the Internet server.

But with the cloud, a third phase has arrived in which the end user can gain "programmatic control" over the powerful server at the other end, if she chooses to. The end user connection is moving toward a peer relationship with the server at the other end.

With programmatic control, the user can tap into and make greater use of all kinds of powerful services that are being built and will be built. Instead of just filling in blanks on a form, the Internet user in the future will send the server instructions on what he would like to do, add his data, select from a list of services, and proceed to manipulate the results. He might even modify the existing services on the fly from his handheld computer, sending the server a bit of his own code telling it what to do. No human has intervened to authorize him to do what he is doing or to explain to him what restrictions apply. On the contrary, if he wants more power, he gets it for a small fee.

Indeed, the user can send the cloud a workload that he's created and instruct it when and how to run that workload.

He can tell it where to store the results and how to save his software application to be run again. Such end users exist today, but they are still relatively skilled programmers who are familiar with the operations of servers on the Internet. But the prerequisites for end user control will shrink rapidly as more sophisticated user interfaces capture the possibilities of the user/cloud relationship. Boxes of checklists, menu selections, dials to power up and power down, and graphs illustrating server levels of strength—the graphical user interface that built up personal computing will soon be handing over more control of Internet server clusters to end users.

With cloud computing, the master/slave relationship has been banished. In its place, a new peer-to-peer relationship is arising between client and server, and some of those servers are found in the most powerful data centers in the world. It's a power shift that will initiate an age of more widely shared resources, more equal access, and powerful servers that follow instructions from remote end users. In the cloud, the common end user is a temporary king over a large domain—if her credit card can support a short list of hourly fees.

This is the change that Ellison and other critics, looking at the big data centers and seeing only a replica of what they've already created, are missing: the self-provisioning aspect of the cloud accompanied by end user programmatic control. Let me offer a short, real-world example.

Amazon.com, in addition to its online store, has pioneered cloud computing as a rentable infrastructure in its data centers called EC2. Outsiders may access its EC2 servers, provision a machine, place a workload on the machine, and get the results back over the Internet. Anyone who creates an account on Amazon's EC2 can put it to work. In effect, it's activated with a swipe of a credit card.

Many businesses are experimenting with Amazon's EC2 to see how it works and what it can do for them, but not much of the enterprise computing workload has moved off businesses' premises into the Amazon infrastructure cloud.

Take the example of drug researcher Pieter Sheth-Voss at Eidetics when he needed to explore the characteristics of a set of 8.6 million patients in order to design a drug test. When he tried to do so on his company's Oracle database system, it took a minute and a half just to find out what portion of the patients were female, and he had hundreds of characteristics that he wanted to explore related to many pieces of data on each patient. He was going to need days of compute time, and he didn't know how to get it.

This skilled director of research was new to the company; Eidetics had just been acquired by Quintiles, a firm that conducts tests for pharmaceutical companies. Quintiles enforced stringent requirements about handling data. Sheth-Voss had no established working relationships with the IT staff in the new company, and he realized to his dismay that it was going to take weeks to get a database server assigned to him.

Instead, he turned to Amazon's EC2, where the database system he needed, Vertica, had already been installed and was available as a service for an hourly charge. It took the researcher 15 minutes to prepare his research program and data, send it to Amazon, and provision a set of servers. The job started at 9 p.m. one evening and finished an hour later.

To Sheth-Voss, the cloud supplied deliverance from a complicated dilemma and allowed him to meet an important deadline for a direct expense that could be covered by many businesses' petty cash funds. Such an outcome would have been unlikely to occur in the past because he would not have been given "programmatic control" of someone else's powerful servers. Hitherto expensive processing, such as analysis of customer buying patterns or how thousands of visitors move around your company's Web site, is suddenly within reach of many who had no means of adding equivalent processing power to their own data center.

If a fast and cheap alternative to Oracle can be found in the cloud, then there may be a method behind Mr. Ellison's putdowns of cloud computing. His company, after all, is heavily invested in the last generation of computing, packaged applications that run in each company's data center. Cloud computing does nothing to further that strategy; in fact, the cloud is a major threat to his business.

As in the example given here, if one researcher with limited computer skills can make use of the cloud, so can many others. In this sense, the cloud is a force that completes something that the PC Revolution started 27 years ago. Computing's end user is now in charge of the resource and will formulate big plans for what to do with it. The master/slave relationship between the PC and the server has been banished. Computing's citizens—or perhaps we should say Netizens—are about to be invested with power over a new domain. The Cloud Revolution is a time of vibrant innovation and upheaval.

This doesn't mean that end users' computers will get bigger and bigger until they're on a par with data center servers. They will continue to get more powerful, but that would have happened anyway. But the servers in the data center will always outweigh them. The cloud will host massive clusters of servers, like Google's, whose combined power dwarfs that of the largest mainframe. The goal isn't equalization in compute cycles between end user and data center. The goal is a peer relationship, where the large can be directed by the small, the mighty are controlled by the meek, and a monumentally expensive server cluster responds to commands from a tiny device held by a person of no social status whatsoever. (If the user is good at cloud computing, then this will change.)

This is the heart of cloud computing, and, for those witnessing the appetite of Facebook users for more services and more computer power, it generates an excitement about the huge possibilities of new services still before us. Sand Hill Road venture capitalists stand ready to fund the visionaries.

In fact, the impetus of cloud computing drives a paradox. The cloud server clusters will keep getting larger, while the end user devices will keep getting smaller. Someday the largest data center on earth may be run by a device that is not as powerful as the long-forgotten original IBM PC from 1983. Several such devices might fit in the palm of one's hand. But no matter how much end user devices shrink, it's essential that they maintain and expand their ability to direct the resources in the cloud.

For now, let's let the technologists argue about what's required for cloud data centers; they can certainly formulate more sophisticated arguments than I can. What we've done is stand that debate on its head. It's not the attributes of the cloud's most conspicuous feature, the Internet server cluster, that matter. It's the nature of the relationship between the end user and those servers—the peer-to-peer relationship—that gives the cloud its defining characteristic and affects businesses the most.

If that's true, then this new machine seems to have a soul. It satisfies a yearning for an equal relationship between the end user and computer power centers that has existed since computing first began. The new machine isn't the sum of an Internet data center's parts. It's the availability—part reality and part illusion—of seemingly endless server cycles for any end user request sent to it.

So far, this door has opened only a crack, and critics such as Ellison can't see past the shadows to the horizon beyond. For that matter, it's very early in the process, and not much in the way of end user empowerment has passed through the opening. Thus, eBay, Gmail, MySpace, Google Apps, Facebook, and Office Live are all just crude early signposts of where cloud computing can take us. Those who understand the change will seize the opportunity and push the door open a little further. But make no mistake, the next generation of computer users and the ones to follow will pass through this portal.

The cloud is going to seize the hopes, the dreams, and the ambitions of people around the world—and supply processing cycles to help make them a reality. It will augment that processing with powerful in-the-cloud services that can perform feats previously considered beyond the reach of all but the most elite. Inside the cloud, the user lives amid an illusion of infinity, resources of endless bounty. For at least a brief period, the illusion is reality. Those who understand that they have the capabilities of the cloud at their disposal and figure out how to put them to use will be revolutionaries for a new day, founders of an all-encompassing, all-embracing digital culture.

2

THE AMORPHOUS CLOUD

Native Americans had no trouble believing that creatures from the spiritual world roamed at will among those of the physical. At night, these visitors became shape shifters, transforming themselves from the coyote, the bear, or the raven into a spirit form, then changing back again at daybreak.

Cloud computing is nothing if not similarly amorphous. The cloud's hard-edged, warehouse-sized data centers accessible on the Internet, filled with seven-foot-tall racks of pizza-box servers, seem concrete enough. But when an individual end user accesses a server in the cloud, the server has the ability to take on or shed processing cycles from CPUs and use more memory or less, as needed. The user's cloud machine expands according to her needs and shrinks when peak processing is over. It may be on one side of the data center one moment and on the opposite the next. The end user hasn't slowed down what she's doing; the shift in servers occurs without her realizing it. In the cloud, the computer becomes a shape shifter. It's not limited by the box it arrived in; instead, it's elastic.

When you need a computing resource to serve you, but you don't know how much of it you're going to need, this special characteristic of the cloud—elasticity—will serve you well.

To see this elasticity in action, take the example of Greg Taylor, senior system engineer at Sony Music Entertainment, who is responsible for the computing infrastructure that supports the Web sites of thousands of recording artists and hundreds of individual artists' online stores. In 2009, Taylor felt that he had adequate monitoring systems and surplus capacity built into his infrastructure. At the MichaelJackson.com store, for example, he could handle the shopping transactions and record comments from 200 shoppers at a time on the store's site.

Upon the star's unexpected death on June 25, 2009, the site was suddenly overwhelmed with people who wanted to buy his music or simply wished to congregate with other grieving fans and leave a comment. Sony Music saw an influx of more than a million people trying to access the Michael Jackson music store over the next 24 hours. Many wanted to post comments, but could not. The servers stayed up, but not everyone who wanted to find album details could be served that information, and indeed, many would-be purchasers could not buy because traffic overwhelmed what was already "a very database intensive" site.

Other surges were felt around the Internet. The Twitter broadcasting site was overwhelmed by users' tweets and slowed to a standstill. TicketMaster in London slowed to a crawl. Yahoo! was staggered by 16.4 million site visitors in the 24 hours, compared to a previous peak of 15.1 million on Election Day.

"Our site became the water cooler for everyone wanting to remember Michael Jackson," Taylor recalled in an interview four months later.

Sony Music's top management told Taylor that it was not acceptable to have traffic trying to reach a company music site and have would-be customers left hanging, with no response from an overwhelmed site. With 200 individual artists' e-commerce sites engaged in capturing both transactions and user feedback, Taylor had a large problem that couldn't be solved in the conventional way: buy a lot more servers, more network bandwidth, and more storage, and throw them at the problem. If he had followed this route, most of that expensive equipment would have sat unused in Sony's own corporate data center. What's a senior system engineer to do?

Taylor has since rearchitected the Michael Jackson store, AC/DC's online store, and other popular artists' sites so that traffic can be split into two streams when necessary: those who are buying music (conducting transactions) and those who are just seeking information. The transactions remain on the core store site hosted on Sony's dedicated servers, but visitors who are seeking read-only content, such as background on an artist and his albums, can be shunted off to the multitenant servers in the cloud. Many cloud customers in addition to Sony Music share those servers, keeping the costs for the music company low.

The cloud service that Taylor chose was Amazon Web Services' Elastic Compute Cloud (EC2). In the future, Sony will build each artist's store in tandem, with an e-commerce site and a related but separate information serving site in EC2. When the e-commerce site starts to get overloaded, the latter can expand to meet nearly any foreseeable traffic count, thanks to the elasticity of the cloud.

As traffic at any artist's Web site builds up to a point where the site can't handle more, new visitors get shunted over to the read-only cloud site, where they can at least find information and identify something that they want to buy. Under the Amazon agreement, cloud servers will scale up to handle as many as 3.5 to 5 million visitors per day, if the occasion ever arises that they need to. In a big traffic spike, a visitor might not be able to purchase an album immediately but will never go away miffed at not being served at all.

The new architecture reflects a changing world where online activities and social networking have taken on added importance. Sony management wants Taylor to be ready for the changes in customer behavior. In the past, there would have been less opportunity for the news of a pop star's death to spread so fast or to result in such a spontaneous outpouring of grief and comment at a well-known music site. If the need arises again, Taylor is in a position to fire up 10 more servers in the cloud as soon as traffic starts to build.

Such elasticity is one of the things that distinguish cloud computing from large corporate data centers. Many data centers include a specially engineered elastic capacity reserved for a select few users, such as major customers who are trying to make purchases on a site that is already busy with browsing visitors. In some cases, more servers are engaged to handle the traffic. But it's also possible for the information seekers to experience delays or even get booted off the site until the buyers have completed their transactions. In the cloud, however, there's no need to turn away desired traffic. Additional "virtual machines" can be fired up quickly to handle all comers.

How to Build an Elastic Cloud Center

In the first chapter, I tried to move the debate away from how large an Internet data center needs to be in order to be included in the cloud, a topic that engineers can argue over, and put the focus on the end users. Now let's move the spotlight in the opposite direction and try to show what the newly empowered end user can do with a data center that's available in the cloud.

As this is being written, Amazon.com itself is 15 years old, but Amazon Web Services' EC2 has been in operation for just three years. As of October 2009, it passed its first-year anniversary of operating as a generally available resource, following two years of operation as a beta, or experimental, facility.

Amazon now offers three different sizes of server to choose from, small, large, and extra large, something like your choices at a Starbucks coffee shop. In addition, Amazon throws in two compute-cycle-intensive variations, which carry out many arithmetical calculations for each step in a program for applications that will require above-average use of CPUs or processors.

Once you've chosen a size, it's still possible to add or subtract capacity by activating or deactivating more servers if the pace at which you want your job to run suddenly demands it. Amazon Web Services includes CloudWatch, where for an hourly fee, operational statistics on the servers you designate to be monitored will be collected. If you subscribe to Cloud-Watch, then you can also receive Auto Scaling, which will take the response time information from CloudWatch and automatically scale up or cut back the number of servers you are using. If you don't want the maximum wait of site visitors to exceed 1.5 seconds, then Auto Scaling will keep enough server availability on hand to maintain that response time.

An additional service that Amazon offers is Elastic Load Balancing, which distributes incoming application traffic across the servers that a customer is operating. This service both spreads the load and detects unhealthy server performance, redistributing the workload around such a server until it can be restored to full operation. Elastic Load Balancing incurs a charge of 2.5 cents per hour, plus 0.8 cent for each gigabyte of data transferred, or 8 cents for every 10 gigabytes through the load balancer. Ten gigabytes is a lot of data; it's equivalent to 100 yards of books on a shelf.

A common case where CloudWatch, Auto Scaling, and Elastic Load Balancing might be useful is when a business is hosting a Web site and doesn't know how much traffic to expect. If the site goes from a few hundred hits an hour to tens of thousands or hundreds of thousands, the site owner can load balance by calling up additional EC2 servers itself, or employ an EC2 management service, such as RightScale, to monitor the situation and perform the task for it. This elasticity comes at a reasonable price; CloudWatch with Auto Scaling results in a charge of 1.5 cents per hour for each EC2 server used.

Other cloud providers offer a similar elasticity of service. Chad Parker, the CEO of Cybernautic, a Web site design firm in Normal, Illinois, was given the task of building a Web site for the Sunday evening hit TV show *Extreme Makeover: Home Edition*. The show was coming to nearby Philo, Illinois, and he knew that he needed more server resources than usual behind the project.

Extreme Makeover travels to a new location each week and shows a home that has been refurbished for a local family with the help of a local builder, friends and neighbors, and hundreds of volunteers, onlookers, and other casual participants. By the time a show airs on a given Sunday evening, several thousand people have had some part in its production, or know someone who has. Parker knew that he had a lot of unpredictable traffic headed his way.

He had a week to get a site up and running that could show text, pictures, and video and be updated frequently. In addition, the multimedia-heavy site would experience severe spikes in traffic when some small event, such as the pouring of the foundation, triggered a response among the event's expanding audience.

Asked what traffic to expect, Conrad Ricketts, *Extreme Makeover*'s executive producer, advised Parker that each site built for the show so far that year had crashed as successive waves of traffic washed over it. "I was told, 'You will need to make sure you have an unlimited supply of beer and pizza for your network administrator,'" recalled Parker when he was interviewed by *InformationWeek* four days after the Philo episode aired. It would be the network administrator's job to reboot the site after each crash. The prediction was that the network administrator would need to be at his post for long periods at a time.

Parker concluded that if he attempted to host the show on his existing servers, the traffic would crash the 200 Web sites of his other existing clients, a prospect that he did not relish. He opted to place the *Extreme Makeover* site in the Rackspace Cloud, a service that guaranteed as much hardware, networking, and storage as the customer needed, no matter how drastically its workload changed.

Contrary to what Parker expected, big waves of traffic hit the site *prior* to the show's October 25, 2009, airing. Parker says he knows that he would not have been ready for those spikes on his own. The newspapers in Bloomington and Champaign wrote stories about the home repair project and the family that would benefit, setting off waves of inquisitive visitors. A follower of the event put up a fan page on Facebook that overnight gained 12,600 fans, most of whom seemed to want to visit the *Extreme Makeover* site several times a day. Parker and his staff were kept busy posting updates, pictures, and stories on the project, updating the site as many as 50 to 60 times per day.

Shortly thereafter, entertainment bloggers in Hollywood wrote about tidbits they had picked up on the upcoming Philo show, generating even more traffic. Visitors to the site spread news of updates over Twitter. Long before the show aired, traffic spiked to heights that Parker would not have conceived possible.

In one 24-hour period, the site had 41,466 visitors, each staying on the site for an average of six minutes and downloading an average of four pages, for a total of 168,873 page views. Going into the project, Parker had conceived of relying on a single dedicated server to host the site. Rackspace Cloud's general manager, Emil Sayegh, was able to marshal dozens of servers—up to 100 were serving the site at certain times—during periods of peak demand, because the combined traffic to all sites in the cloud is automatically monitored, and managers keep a constant surplus of capacity on standby at all times. As *Extreme Makeover* ate into that surplus, Rackspace fired up more servers to stay ahead of demand. The elastic cloud expanded to meet the need as it materialized.

To Parker's surprise, traffic was steady as the show aired Sunday evening and dropped off soon afterward. The spikes had been prior to the show because participants in the project, their families and friends, and interested onlookers were anticipating what the show would reveal and wanted to be the first to know.

Parker says that the experience has convinced Cybernautic to drop its current form of computing, renting servers from a service provider, and to move his clients' 200 Web sites into the multitenant Rackspace cloud, where customers share servers but always have enough capacity to go around.

"I don't need to worry anymore about whether I need to add another server. The cloud automatically scales to match what I need," Parker said.

Much of the excitement about the cloud reflects this understanding of its elastic nature, its ability to scale up and down for nearly any kind of business. Building elasticity into the corporate data center used to be handled by buying and installing servers until you had more capacity than you actually needed—an expensive proposition. With the cloud, it's suddenly possible for a small company, like Cybernautic, to do everything that a big company would do. Best of all, you pay only for the resources that you use, as opposed to buying and installing resources that you might use but that will sit idle most of the time.

Amazon charges 8.5 cents an hour to run a Linux server or 12 cents an hour for a Windows server; Rackspace charges 1.5 cents an hour per Linux server. Additional charges are incurred for load balancing, auto scaling, and so on. In general, cloud prices are deemed to be as low as or lower than the charges arising from the most economical corporate data center operation. The economies of scale built into the cloud give it an ability to adjust on the fly for end users who need it— both large and small businesses—and an ability to maintain low charges.

WHAT DOES A CLOUD
DATA CENTER COST?

Microsoft is building six data centers to power Azure and its other online services, two in North America (Chicago and San Antonio, Texas), two in Europe (Dublin, Ireland, and a second site to be determined), and two in Asia (Hong Kong and Singapore). The two centers in each region are linked and are probably designed to back each other up, a common practice among cloud providers. In fact, Google is believed to have constructed at least 12 data centers around the world and various other supporting facilities. Only Google knows the degree to which these data centers back each other up, but by design, the Google search engine seems to be always available around the world.

Building paired backup sites is a measure of how heavily the early suppliers of cloud computing have invested to be at the forefront. From public documents citing the permits for Microsoft cloud centers, two of them cost about $1 billion. But Moore's law, which asserts that the power of computer chips doubles every two years, will keep reducing the cost of building the equivalent of today's cloud data centers. Indeed, cloud computing in the form of the containerized data center, with a 20- or 40-foot shipping container dropped off at a site, plugged in as a unit, and 2,000 to 2,500 computers coming to life together, is going to drive down data center costs.

(continues)

For its part, Amazon was building a cloud data center complex along the Columbia River in Boardman, Oregon, but work was halted temporarily in 2009 because of the recession. This location is advantageous because wholesale electricity is readily available from nearby hydroelectric generation. The 117,000-square-foot facility is surrounded by an eight-foot chain-link fence topped with barbed wire and is estimated to cost $100 million, once equipped. It is expected to be followed by two more such buildings.

Further, cloud provider Terremark has built a networked data center for secure government use in Culpepper, Virginia, behind a 12-foot berm, blastproof walls, 250 motion sensor cameras, and a guard at a reinforced front gate, at a price of $250 million.

In a few years, when true competition kicks in to supply cloud computing, Microsoft's 12.5 cents per hour for a small Windows server and Amazon Web Services' 12 cents per hour will look less like a reasonable rate. Prices are low, and they will be driven even lower. How low can they go? Probably to the cost of the electricity needed to run the computer plus some very low additional charge per hour, say from one cent down to tenths of a cent.

Many businesses will see the benefits of such data centers and become users, but they will try to do so without getting locked into a service pattern dictated by one vendor.

If more resources are needed, the chances that the cloud can summon them are high. It would be expensive for cloud providers to keep massive amounts of surplus facilities sitting around unused day after day waiting for a rare spike. But the cloud doesn't have to do that because it is a multitenant facility, with many customers using the same servers, and in some cases the same software. The cloud managers make an educated guess at how much surplus capacity is safe to maintain; their advanced load-balancing systems can anticipate need, adding more servers for more direct power, while at the same time moving workloads around to underutilized servers.

The cloud's operations managers base their estimate of what constitutes a safe surplus on the analysis of server logs and historical patterns from monitoring the servers' total workload. Managers also hope that not every cloud customer will create a major spike at the same time, an admittedly rare possibility. This appearance of expandable capacity for any single end user is to some extent an illusion. Somewhere, as with all material things, there is a limit to how many major spikes could be met at one time in any given cloud data center. But with thousands or tens of thousands of customers, what is the likelihood that the cloud provider will experience a surge in need from a majority of its customers at the same time?

In the normal course of operations, multiple customer spikes are infrequent and, fortunately, spikes rarely travel in herds if the customers are varied in their business makeup. A cloud's monitoring system can show warning flags, send alerts, or sound alarms; somewhere behind the automated system is a management console with a human watching. However, the cloud's own monitoring system is capable of anticipating need and quickly firing up additional "virtual machines" as needed. By doing its computing in the cloud, a business like Cyber-nautic can grow its Web site business quickly, without hiring a burgeoning IT staff or undergoing the expense of construct-ing an overbuilt data center with a large margin of surplus capacity. At the same time, a large enterprise could siphon off demanding but noncritical jobs in its data center by sending them to the cloud and reducing the capacity that it needs to keep on hand.

The Cloud Is Different from What's Gone Before

Much of what we've covered so far could theoretically apply to older, specialized forms of computing as well. The IBM main-frame frequently had a capacity surplus for the workloads that it processed, and it could juggle workloads with ease. For ex-ample, IBM Sysplex, a cluster of mainframes, generated enor-mous capacities.

Many universities, including Cornell, the University of Illi-nois at Urbana-Champaign, and the University of Texas at Austin, have built out a supercomputer from a cluster of small machines. The Department of Energy is a major supercom-puter builder. NASA, NOAA, and the National Laboratories have also linked arms with industry leaders to build high-performance computing clusters for use by researchers and scientists. Are these supercomputers automatically considered part of the cloud as well?

No, they are not, at least not yet. Cloud computing connotes a business model of elastic resources being available on demand to whomever needs them, without special qualifications, at low hourly rates. All of the examples just given were previously reserved for a select few. Now, the cloud makes elasticity available as part of a commodity service that is available to every type of business, large or small. That cloud model dictates a type of data center architecture that both can be quickly expanded and is cost-effective for the resources put into it. In cloud computing, building a cloud-based data center on the network out of the most reliable but lowest-cost parts appears to be a special skill.

For there to be a PC revolution, Intel, AMD, and a handful of other chip suppliers had to master the art of producing microprocessors cheaply and make the process reliable as it ran through millions of repetitions. These manufacturers pushed forward the performance of their initially weak designs at a rapid rate. "In the early '90s, the continuing rise of microprocessor performance made itself felt," wrote Gregory Pfister, an IBM researcher who summed up the trend in his 1995 book *In Search of Clusters*.

Cloud data centers are built out of what are essentially personal computer parts, with memory, microprocessors, and disk drives that have been perfected through the process of being mass produced by the million, with ruthless competition weeding out any company that is prone to produce faulty parts. A desktop or laptop microprocessor isn't much to behold by itself, but when microprocessors are combined into four-, six-, or eight-CPU servers, and thousands of these servers are clustered together in a cloud data center, they represent a new type of computing resource, one that combines an ability to deliver either standard or high performance at prices that reflect low-cost parts. These individual microprocessors are referred to as x86 chips, and they are produced on a scale that dwarfs the output of any of the high-end processors used in IBM mainframes or large Unix servers.

It's possible to build a large computer or computer cluster without using x86 parts. For instance, HP's Superdome and Sun Microsystems' UltraSPARC 10000 Starfire use high-end server processors that pack more processing punch into each CPU but lack the economies of scale possessed by the cloud data centers built from x86 parts. But as of now, there are no clouds based on high-end CPUs. It's not in a definition anywhere, but cloud computing connotes mass-produced parts assembled into massive units delivering new economies of scale.

Clouds are a form of cluster computing, and so far only a small handful of companies have gained the knowledge of how to build out very large clusters for general public use. These companies include Amazon Web Services, Google's App Engine, Microsoft's Azure cloud, the Rackspace Cloud, Sun Microsystems (now part of Oracle), IBM, Yahoo!, eBay, and Facebook. Other large Internet companies have also built big data centers with x86 parts, but so far they are not available to the public for on-demand, general-purpose, cloud-style computing uses.

A High Hurdle to Get into the Cloud

If cloud computing is so exciting and inexpensive, why aren't there more cloud suppliers?

At the heart of this new phase of computing is the dark art of building clusters. Clusters are servers that are tied together to make use of their combined power. Each computer in the cluster needs to be linked to every other computer through a cluster interface (called the cluster network) because it may need the results of the other computers' processing. This sounds simple, but in an interview several years ago, Gregory Pfister told me that there was no clear blueprint for building clusters. It's more like going back to maps of the world in the Middle Ages. You travel a certain distance along known paths, then knowledge ends and a drawing in the margins tells you *hic sunt dracones* (here be dragons).

When every computer needs to be connected to every other computer, a lot of overhead is created by the need to track what each node is doing and where data is located. Once the connections are made, all the cluster builder has to do is provide cluster management software that can decide how to distribute, track, and keep synchronized the work being done by each node in the cluster and what each should do next. If one node changes the data, it's important that every other node have some way of discovering that change before it goes ahead and acts on the same data, lest the integrity of the data be lost. All this activity has a price. It adds to the overall amount of processing that needs to be done to accomplish a task. The bigger the cluster, the more overhead generated to manage it.

Cloud data centers have overcome the barriers to building large clusters that continue to scale upward in processing power as more servers are added. They may lose a small portion of that power; perhaps 10 or 15 percent of each server's processing has to be sacrificed to overhead. But a great deal of the power of each added server gets added to the collective power of the cluster. A lot of design skill has gone into allowing the cluster to scale out as the number of nodes grows into the thousands. Google, Amazon.com, Microsoft, IBM, Rackspace, and other suppliers appear to have mastered the art of building clusters for public cloud computing purposes.

Writing in 1995, Pfister with foresight concluded: "Suddenly, large but practical-sized agglomerations of microprocessors didn't just equal big machine performance or provide it more cheaply. They clearly became the way to exceed even the biggest and superest computer speeds by large amounts."

There are many people in Silicon Valley who would be building cloud computers—small clusters—in their basements at night, if only it were easy to do. All too soon the would-be cluster builder reaches the territory where *hic sunt dracones*, and the performance of his cluster is consumed by its own design.

If today's cloud suppliers have avoided this pitfall, how big are their clusters? Yahoo! runs one type of cloud software, called Hadoop, a data analysis system, on clusters of 4,000 computers. But the size of a single cluster is no longer the point. The cloud supplier of the future will build a series of data centers around the world, putting compute power close to multiple world population centers, and let one data center supplement another, perhaps as part of the world goes to sleep and another part wakes up.

I previously estimated that Google operates 500,000 to 600,000 servers in its 12 data centers and auxiliary processing facilities around the world (no one outside Google knows for sure) and has plans to manage up to one million or more. (As this was being written, a report, unconfirmed by Google, circulated among knowledgeable server and software suppliers that Google crossed the one million server mark in 2009.) At some point, the server count becomes irrelevant. What matters is how effectively these masses of computers can stay up and running, meet massive user demand, and survive faults and mishaps in their own operation and natural disasters outside them. The day may come when a giant cluster will fail, but its users won't notice. The other clusters linked to it should prove able to take on its workload, with only a slight impact on overall user response times. That would be an acceptable trade-off in cloud computing.

Nevertheless, the size achieved by an individual cluster has reached a very large scale. The cluster dragon has been slain, or at least his all-consuming wrath has been circumvented. And a new management layer is thrown over the whole cluster that requires few people to keep it running, a major contributor to the new economies of scale. If these new clusters can be expanded indefinitely, then much of the cloud's mystique revolves around the potential new consumer services that such large facilities might enable.

The Google Cloud Example:
How the Cloud Runs without Stopping

We've noted a couple of features of the cloud data center that make its elasticity possible, but let's take a quick look at the underlying architecture of the cloud to see how it can constantly expand its capacity. Google has supplied some details of how they are engineered.

For its servers, Google doesn't buy an existing piece of x86 hardware from a major supplier, even though dozens of types are available. On the contrary, it builds its servers itself from standard x86 parts. That's probably because it's looking for a particular type of cost/benefit ratio in the many servers it operates. It's vital that it achieve the lowest cost possible on a server design it is going to replicate thousands of times. The corporate data center tends to address this problem differently. Many companies buy the most reliable server available with built-in redundant parts, so that the failure of a component doesn't bring the server down. Google strips out such redundancies from its server design, such as double fans for ensured cooling or backup power supplies, even though the server would operate longer if each of these common causes of component failure had a redundant part. Such features add cost that gets multiplied many thousands of times in Google data centers.

What a Google server has that other servers don't is a simple lead-acid battery attached to the power supply that will give a server a life-support system for a short period if its power supply unit dies. During that life extension, I suspect that Google operation managers are alerted, the failing server is identified, and its workload is moved elsewhere before the battery is exhausted. I suspect but do not know that all this happens automatically. A human somewhere notes the server outage. At some point during a regular maintenance sweep, the power supply unit is replaced and the server is brought back online, or perhaps the entire server is replaced when it reaches a certain age.

Google officials have talked about how they've designed their data center expecting such component failures. When there are tens of thousands of servers working together, such failures, which are infrequent for the home computer user, start to occur on a regular basis. Disk drives fail, power supplies fail, network interface cards fail, other components seize up, and the server grinds to a halt.

In a paper outlining many aspects of the cloud data center, Urs Holzle, senior vice president of engineering at Google, and Luiz Barroso, Google distinguished engineer, say, "An application (such as a search engine) running across thousands of machines may need to react to failure conditions on an hourly basis." Holzle and Barroso have given us a major clue to the rise of cloud computing: it achieves new economies of scale yet remains broadly available to multitenant users because it's being managed by software, not humans, and it achieves fault tolerance in that software, not the hardware.

For example, Google has designed its search engine operation with the expectation that one or more single nodes within the cluster will fail. Rather than try to build infallibility into the hardware, it has kicked the responsibility upstairs to the software governing the cluster. Software can supply fault tolerance, or the ability to cope with the failure of any single component, by routing work around that failure and redoing it in a separate component within the cloud.

Fault tolerance has always been expensive to solve in hardware. Google uses the cheapest highly reliable parts and lives with failures as they occur. Corporate data centers pay a high price for the reliability they buy in hardware, but it's worth it to them not to have critical business systems go down. Solving the problem in software makes it a simple task to add a hardware server without a lot of advance preparation. In the unlikely event that the server fails early in its normal life span, the cluster can cope.

Yahoo! recently offered a more specific example of fault tolerance in software that it has implemented in its cloud-style database system, Hadoop, running on clusters of up to 4,000 servers at a time and 25,000 servers in all. Hadoop sorts through data gained from each active site on the Web. Without Hadoop, sorting the results of a complete Web crawl took so long that new sites appeared on the Web before the task could be completed, and the results were badly out of date. With Hadoop, the indexing of the Web can be done in 73 hours, so a Yahoo! Web search is only three days behind the actual state of the Web.

Google, Amazon.com, and now Yahoo!, as it embarks on its own use of cloud data centers internally (a private cloud), have all adopted a design principle from the Internet itself. The Department of Defense, through its Defense Advanced

Research Projects Agency (DARPA), wanted a network that would survive a nuclear attack; what it got was the birth of the Internet. The routers on the Internet detect when a router in the next network segment isn't working and automatically route around it. Likewise, when a server in a cloud data center fails, the managing software routes the workload elsewhere and doesn't send that server anything more to do until it's fixed.

A fault-tolerant data center made from inexpensive parts used to be an oxymoron. At one time, Tandem Computers achieved fault tolerance, but only by running identical computers side by side doing the same work, so that one could fail without an impact on the business. Now fault tolerance is one of the secrets behind elasticity. If adding hardware is a simple, low-cost task, then hardware can be pulled on line as needed. If failures occur, as they inevitably do, they can be managed routinely and the data center will continue functioning. This is a central principle of what Holzle and Barroso called "The Data Center as a Computer: An Introduction to the Design of Warehouse-Scale Machines," their Synthesis Lecture on Computer Architecture at the University of Wisconsin, Madison.

One additional example: as noted before, the large cluster needs an interconnect that ties it into the other machines in the cluster. Many have wondered how Google's warehouse-scale machine achieves this, and have assumed that it used the highest-speed interconnects available to achieve the speeds that it does. High-speed interconnects, however, are also the most expensive method, violating the principle that the cloud data center must be built with reliable but inexpensive parts. Infiniband networks can transport data at 40 gigabits per second. High-end Ethernet transports it at 10 gigabits per second, and these were my candidates for Google's interconnect fabric.

Holzle and Barroso say that this can't be so. Infiniband costs $500 to $1,000 extra per port, they write. Large-scale Ethernet moves data at 10 gigabits per second, "but again, at a cost of hundreds of dollars per server. The alternative is low-cost fabrics from commodity Ethernet switches." I don't know the brand name or capacity of the Google cluster switching fabric. But a highly reliable 1-gigabit Ethernet switch, for example, costs $148.

The interconnect, like the servers themselves, is built out of the most proven mass-produced parts. Elasticity is related to this economy of scale. If you haven't mastered the art of building the big server cluster, you will find it hard to deliver "elastic" service. Remember, you've got to do so within the cloud business model, which demands low prices. How low? As low as your competitors can go. It's a tough trade-off. In the cloud, elasticity is inevitably tied to implementing massive economies of scale.

Many simple computers built of similar parts can be managed by fewer people. One management interface and a layer of system management software can scale up to many units, noting which ones are functioning properly and which ones are showing signs of heating up, slowing down, or experiencing malfunctioning parts.

The cloud data center is a cluster different from any that we've seen before. The fact that this resource is available to many users at highly economical rates is part of the excitement of cloud computing.

We still haven't touched on one of the most important ways in which the cloud becomes elastic, however, and that's virtualization. The impact of virtualization has been so great that it's the subject of the next chapter. But we know that elasticity is built into the design of the cloud data center. It's elasticity that is responsible for the illusion that we are connected to a boundless resource, capable of processing the most demanding job we can conjure up. It's an outstanding feature of cloud computing.

Elasticity is responsible for much of the excitement surrounding cloud computing. If we can process anything that we want, then what do we want to process? Whether the cloud user is an individual or a business, a new opportunity is unfolding. A convergence of technologies, evolutionary in form, looks more and more revolutionary in scope. Critics are inclined to say that there's nothing in the cloud that they haven't seen before. Some critic, I suspect, said the same thing about the printing press.

Cloud computing takes a set of technologies that have been already proved elsewhere and leverages them to generate new economies of scale and new end user services. Everyone is fascinated with the size of the cloud data centers—eight football fields across, one analyst said. But some observers are intrigued with what the end user is going to do with this resource. Amid the data center's whirring fans and grinding disks, I keep hearing an echo of the PC Revolution. It may be just an illusion that we can do anything we want to "in the cloud," but it's an illusion that the cloud is likely to sustain far into the future.

3

VIRTUALIZATION CHANGES EVERYTHING

Throughout the natural world, when a creature confronts a challenging situation, its hair stands on end or its quills are extended, or its cheeks puff out. Animals that normally walk on all fours stand upright and snap their jaws. It's the oldest trick of evolution: make yourself appear larger than you are, and perhaps a rival, a predator, or some other form of intractable problem will go away.

I've already referred to the illusion of endless power that the cloud data center imparts. It has a whole raft of tricks to achieve this larger-than-life result, but in challenging cloud situations, it's virtualization that leverages servers to make them appear larger than they really are.

The real secret of the cloud's economies of scale, elastic operation, and smooth availability to remote end users is not just a big data center composed of PC parts, the use of Web services standards, or the automated ability to balance workloads. It's primarily virtualization.

There is no definition of a cloud—not even my own in Chapter 1—that requires the servers in a cloud data center to be virtualized, but nevertheless, in the long run, no public, multitenant cloud is going to be competitive without it. Amazon Web Services' Elastic Compute Cloud (EC2), the leader in cloud computing, relies on virtualization. The workloads running in it are based on Amazon's version of the open source code Xen virtual machine. But what is virtualization?

Virtualization in its simplest form is the process of taking a physical machine and subdividing it through software into the equivalent of several discrete machines. While these machines operate independently, they share the hardware resources of a single server without impinging on each other. Computers of many brands and stripes can be subdivided this way, beginning with the IBM mainframe. IBM invented the concept of virtualization. But virtualization has had its biggest impact on x86 computers, the popular mass-produced models that use Intel and AMD chips. These chips are found in everything from lightweight netbooks to laptops, desktops, and powerful data center servers. These computers typically run Windows, Linux, Solaris for x86, or Netware as an operating system.

Virtualization boosts computers' productivity at a time when their capacities are being expanded rapidly. In effect, virtualization has made servers built with PC-style parts the basis for the general-purpose cloud data center, such as EC2, because through virtualization, a cloud service can place many users on one machine without danger that they will trespass on each other or see each other's data. The overseer of the virtual machines is the hypervisor, a superb automated allocator of resources among competing demands.

One hypervisor sits on each server running several virtual machines; it understands the division of hardware resources set up by the human system administrator, who assigns each virtual machine a share of the computer's random access memory, central processing unit (CPU) cycles, network bandwidth, and disk storage. Then it referees the competing demands for these resources. The computer that is running multiple virtual machines is often referred to as the host. The virtual machines themselves are often referred to as the guests of the host. The host will be powered by its own operating system, such as Linux or Windows Server, but each guest has its own operating system as well. This all sounds confusing at first, but it works extremely well. Each virtual machine behaves just like a physical machine in terms of its ability to run a business application, and often there is only a small performance penalty for running ten applications per server instead of just one.

Virtualization is one of the key technologies that gives the cloud its elastic quality, so that a user can enlist support from many servers and, conversely, many users can receive services from the same server. Intel and AMD are routinely delivering CPUs, the central brain of the computer, that consist of four cores. Each core is a full microprocessor in itself; four of them together occupy one microprocessor socket at the heart of the server. The number is a moving target; some 6-core CPUs are now available, and the manufacturers are headed for 8 and 12 cores soon. The numbers won't stop there.

VMware is the market leader in virtualization. In late 2009, I asked VMware's vice president of enterprise desktop marketing, Patrick Harr, how many active end users, each using her own virtual machine, a core can support. On the latest generation of Intel processors, called Nehalem (Xeon 5500), or AMD's latest Opteron chips, the number has doubled to sixteen per core, he said. A typical low-cost server has two CPUs, each with four cores, for a total of eight cores. Such a machine can support up to 128 end users, each in an individual virtual machine that is able to use memory, CPU cycles, disk drive, and input/output (I/O) on the network.

Another typical configuration for a low-cost server is four CPUs occupying four sockets, with each CPU consisting of four cores. To complete the math, the 16 cores on such a server are capable of supporting 256 end users, each in his own virtual machine. These are not high-end servers, but rather basic building block servers, something like those described in Chapter 2. These basic servers are likely to be heavily equipped with memory and input/output devices, the network interface devices that move network and storage data on and off the computer, to support so many users, which in the end puts them in a different class from "commodity." But in other respects, they resemble the most cost-effective hardware designs on the market.

Google figured out how to build such plain vanilla cloud servers ahead of the rest of the marketplace and thus launched into manufacturing its own. Over the last two years, Dell has expressed interest in supplying the needs of cloud builders and has shown an understanding of what those special needs would be.

The rapid expansion of the number of cores per CPU has to some extent caught the traditional data center by surprise. For many years, corporate data centers have usually been organized around a principle of one application on one server, for ease of administration and avoidance of application conflicts. Where that's still the case, many cores sit idle, as the application's needs are met by only one or two cores. AMD says it will produce Opteron chips with 16 cores in 2012. What is to be done with all those cores?

Virtualization's hypervisor loves cores for their ability to pour out CPU cycles. Host machines in the cloud are running multiple virtual machines that demand more and more CPU cycles. Multiple-core servers and multiuser clouds: it's a match—if not one made in heaven, then at least one that was previously difficult to achieve on the ground. Virtual machines run in the cloud, and with the refreshing of server hardware that's currently under way, twice as many can run on inexpensive hardware. This process of being able to run more and more virtual machines appears to be accelerating.

Circuits are still shrinking on the chips—Intel has started fabricating chips with circuits that are 32 billionths of a meter thick, which speeds performance. Clock speeds may not be going up as fast as they used to, but increases in the number of cores more than compensates. The most recent generation of Intel x86 servers continuously runs two processes at a time on each core—that is, it executes two separate sequences of instructions, a trick that was formerly reserved for server chip designs, not those produced for "personal computing." This is another reason that virtualization is thriving on the x86 architecture. Virtualization plus x86 has become a cloud builder and a driver of the cloud's extraordinary economies of scale.

But there's a discrepancy to explain. The discussion with Harr concerned individual end users and their virtual machine needs. What if the customer of the cloud service is a business, and it's running a business application? That's a bigger task, because many end users use a business application at the same time, so there's a higher demand for CPU cycles.

Skilled implementers in cloud data centers are already running 10 to 12 business applications on one server in virtual machines. So virtualization of business applications has the effect of consolidating what used to require 10 to 12 physical servers into 1. But server experts say that the now current generation of servers based on faster chips, such as Intel's Nehalem (Xeon 5500), will also double this number. In fact, many believe that it will be common for a standard x86 server to host 30 virtual machines, each running a business application, by the end of 2010.

Highly skilled virtualization implementers, such as Accenture, which manages enterprise IT on an outsourced basis, already run 60 virtual machines (VMs) per server through the techniques they've learned, which include offloading the server's virtual machine I/O to the network. Accenture has successfully tested 100 VMs per server on its existing generation of hardware. As it refreshes its data center, it could be possible for a practiced implementer, such as Accenture, to run upward of 120 virtual machines per server, and probably more. And if Accenture can do it, so can the cloud providers.

The x86 architecture is thus being put in a commanding position to dominate cloud computing, if ways can be found to automate the management of large numbers of x86 machines at one time.

Having multiplied the productivity of such servers, virtualization weighs in again in providing the means to manage large numbers of servers from a single console. This is another match-up with the needs of the cloud. For example, if a virtual machine has been assigned a "virtual" CPU, one gigabyte of memory, and 33 percent of a network interface card (an I/O device that plugs into a server to manage its network traffic), these resources might be sufficient to keep a small Web site running smoothly while being hosted in the cloud. But what if something unexpected happens and traffic builds on the site beyond any level envisioned, as happened with Sony Music's Michael Jackson store? It would be possible to quickly double or triple the resources of the virtual machine by taking them from the unused portion of the host server. Or a management system could move other virtual machines off the server to free up those resources, a process called live migration. To their end users, the virtual machines appear to continue running even as they're being moved, making it easier for managers to react to traffic spikes by moving VMs around. As another alternative, the virtual machine manager could decide to move the virtual machine that was starving for more CPU to a different physical server where more cycles were available, again without interrupting the operation of the VM as far as its end users were concerned.

Virtualization gives the cloud data center manager an arsenal of weapons with which to attack the problem of balancing his systems against demand and dividing up resources. Virtualization to a great extent breaks the hard boundaries that used to surround each physical machine and substitutes a more plastic resource for the cloud operations manager. He can mold that resource with more flexibility than his predecessors could. In the cloud, where he needs to maintain the illusion of unlimited resources for users, the operations manager has ample cause to enlist the virtual machine management console and view all his servers through it.

Managing by Moving Things Around

Two or three years ago, the notion of moving a running application would have struck many professional IT managers as dangerous, if not preposterous, because of the potential for a crashed process. But today the virtual machine's ability to conduct a "live migration," or a move from one physical server to another, while running is accepted as a reliable data center technique. Not that it doesn't still inspire a bit of awe. One IT manager said that when he showed end users how he could move their running virtual machines without disruption, it appeared to confer on him "godlike" powers, in the observers' eyes.

It's not a big mystery how this is possible. In effect, the hypervisor figures out the part of an application that the virtual machine is about to use and leaves that part running on the existing server, while moving all the other parts to a different physical server. The hypervisor moves the data that the application doesn't need at the moment to the same server, then, when all is ready, it suspends the VM's operation, moves the last 10 to 20 percent of the application code to the new location, and resumes operation. It happens at the speed of light, in a few thousandths, or at most hundredths, of a second. A perceptive end user might notice a slight pause in operation, but most IT managers say that the shift is imperceptible to most users.

Today, that migration can be performed by a cloud system administrator or by automated software that's been authorized to act under certain conditions. A service-level agreement between the cloud supplier and the customer sets an allowable time for applications to respond to users. If that response time is threatened, the automatic management system activates more resources one way or another so that the application servers can quickly solve the problem.

In addition to the commercial systems that are capable of doing this, some free open source code systems, such as VMware's Hyperic HQ management system, are giving cloud customers the ability to peer into their cloud virtual machine's operation and deduce on their own what's going on. This ability passes the ability to make management decisions by remote control back to the end user, giving the end user even more power.

Those decisions can be based on the end user's priorities, not the cloud's. A business tenant of the cloud can determine who is a high-priority user—say a regular large customer who pays on time—and give that user more resources when he appears on the site, at the expense of customers who just browse or those with poor credit ratings and payment practices. Those users get moved to more heavily taxed hosts and endure longer response times.

So far we've been examining how virtualization makes it easier to convert a big cloud data center into a multitenant facility, improving its ease of management and multiplying its already powerful economies of scale. Next, we'll look at how virtualization also smooths the path for end users to use the cloud.

Mobile Workload Packages: The Virtual Appliance

Virtualization also affects the other end of cloud computing, the end user with a workload that she wishes to prepare and launch in the cloud. To realize what the end user does with virtualization, it's necessary to delve a little deeper into how virtualization changes the software that the end user is dealing with.

The historic role of the operating system is to hear the application's calls for hardware services, such as an accounting system calling for two numbers to be added together, and pass that request for service to the hardware, which then performs the task. The operating system understands the instruction set of the hardware that it's running on. Thus Windows, Linux, and Solaris for x86 all understand what to do when the accounting system says, "Add these two numbers"; they pass the numbers to the "adder" that is etched into the processor and return the result to the application.

The role of the operating system changed, however, when virtualization's hypervisor appeared on the scene. In 1999, VMware's former chief scientist, Mendel Rosenblum, demonstrated in a product, VMware Workstation, that he had captured the ability to mimic Intel's complicated and proprietary x86 hardware instruction set in software. This had long been thought to be impossible, or at least so difficult that it wouldn't be cost-effective to try. Four years after Workstation came on the scene, the feat was duplicated in the Computer Laboratory at the University of Cambridge in the Xen Project led by Ian Pratt.

Both of these projects have led to hypervisors—the virtual machine supervisors—that are capable of telling hardware what to do based on what an application requires. Without going deeper into the nuts and bolts of hypervisors, this enables the hypervisor to displace the operating system. Virtualization lifts the operating system up a layer and slides the hypervisor in underneath it. Now the hypervisor takes over the role of talking to the hardware, leaving the operating system to talk only to the application and pass its needs down to the hypervisor.

The most immediate result of the operating system's displacement is that it breaks what had hitherto been the surest of bonds, that between the business application and a particular piece of hardware.

This discussion might sound academic, but this change is what provides flexibility and power to the users of cloud computing. Applications are computing's workhorses; they power the processes that keep businesses running. They contain the business logic that gets work done for the end user, whether it's the chief financial officer, the factory floor manager, or the youngest rep on the sales force.

Applications and hardware used to be so tightly welded together that corporate data center managers hated to have to migrate an application off its existing hardware. Often it had been running on the same machine for eight or ten years. But gains in hardware performance are so swift that such migrations become necessary after an extended period. That meant that the application needed to be tested with a new version of the operating system geared to new hardware. It often meant many finite adjustments to the application itself and uncertainty over whether it would continue to run flawlessly. Everything might still have the same name, such as Xeon hardware, the Windows operating system, and the General Accounting application, but in fact thousands of little changes had gone on underneath the covers during those eight to ten years. At the end of a long and painful migration path, with the new system configured and the application adjustments made, the application could still fail. The result inevitably was upset users calling the data center, if not calling for IT managers' heads. And CEOs, COOs, and CFOs sometimes joined in.

With the tie between the application and a particular piece of hardware broken, the traditional data center benefits by being able to upgrade its hardware but continue using the old version of the application, sidestepping the need to migrate it. Instead, the application runs in a virtual machine with the old operating system. Remember that both the virtual machine and the virtual machine's host have their own operating system. They may have started out at the same time and with the same version, but now they part ways. The hypervisor beneath the virtual machine is indifferent to which version of an operating system it is talking to. It continues to direct the hardware instruction set on what to do, just as before.

This characteristic becomes extremely useful in a cloud data center. For one thing, a multitenant server is going to need to process the needs of varied end users. Some may send a workload under Windows, others under Linux, and still others under Solaris. The hypervisor doesn't care. It will run them all side by side on the same physical server, giving cloud suppliers a great deal of flexibility in choosing how they wish to manage their resources and which environments they wish to support.

More important, the end user of the cloud now has the means of packaging the application and the version of the operating system with which it runs best as a single set of files, something that is currently called a "virtual appliance." The end user in this case is usually a skilled programmer or IT manager acting on behalf of business end users. What's important is that this set of files can be transferred over the Internet to whatever cloud service the IT manager chooses. Unfortunately, different clouds accept different file formats, but a reasonably informed IT manager can cope with specific requirements and cast the virtual appliance in the correct format. By freeing itself from dependence on an underlying piece of hardware, a business application gains mobility and the chance to thrive in the cloud. Today the primary cloud of choice is EC2, running virtual machines as Amazon Machine Images. Tomorrow it may be any of the dominant virtualization formats, including VMware's Virtual Machine Disk format (VMDK) or Microsoft and Citrix Systems' Virtual Hard Disk (VHD). Clouds are being built to accept virtual appliances in those and other formats.

If the end user has registered with the cloud and has a credit card account, then the workload will be accepted and automatically run. Without human intervention, EC2 can execute this process, apply its automated billing system to charge the user's account, and send the user notice that his job has been completed and is stored in the Amazon S3 storage location that he previously rented.

Virtual Appliances

A virtual appliance is an application and operating system combination, looking for a suitable hardware location in which to run on the Internet. It's tailor-made for the cloud.

How complicated is it to build a virtual appliance? Chances are that a developer who is skilled in the conventions of Web services and the virtualization world can do it today, and anyone with scripting language skills or basic programming skills has a good shot at completing the process. Those who are willing to can study the online information available and use the free tools available, such as rBuilder from rPath, to help the process along.

The question might be, who will turn into skilled builders of virtual appliances? In fact, rPath is a firm that specialized in creating them, but the skill is unlikely to be limited to any particular entity for very long. Rather, it's going to become a general skill wherever expertise in an application teams up with expertise in the operating system that runs it. Today such expertise is present on many IT staffs, whose members assign system administrators to manage a few servers running particular applications and operating systems. This is a labor-intensive approach. In the future practice of cloud computing, such skills at one company might be recognized by others and not duplicated elsewhere. Instead, many other companies might adopt skillfully produced virtual appliances for a small fee. Virtual appliances are a way of capturing the best expertise available and sharing it broadly, as opposed to every IT staff trying to produce its own. The main point is that virtualization plus cloud computing means that the productivity of the IT staff can be multiplied, if it is managed right. Develop the in-house expertise that you really need to run proprietary processes, and shop for other expertise that's available elsewhere. A smart builder will strip the operating system down to only the parts needed by the application.

Up to this point, Windows, Unix, and Linux have been general-purpose operating systems, needing to be able to meet the needs of thousands of different applications. Each operating system is loaded with features and functions that allow it to cover the whole gamut of potential application needs. What if the operating system could be reduced to only what a particular application needs? If the best experts built a virtual appliance, they could strip away the unneeded parts of the operating system, particularly with Linux, which lends itself to becoming a slimmed-down system specialized to run a particular appliance. (Windows and Unix are less amenable to being shorn of parts; they have many dependencies between their moving parts.) Such a stripped-down operating system would make the application run faster because the stack of all operating system code sequences and modules has gotten smaller, and the controlling intelligence has less to hunt through to find what it needs.

The virtual appliance can be smaller than the original operating system/application combination. It can move from point to point over the Internet faster and run faster in the cloud, saving its owner money. This is another paradox of cloud computing. Virtualization inevitably imposes overhead on operations because the hypervisor has intervened between the operating system and the hardware, adding a step in the passing of instructions to the hardware. At the same time, virtualization enables the operating system to be stripped down and function on behalf of one specific application rather than many. The ultimate result is likely to be, at least as expressed by rPath founder Billy Marshall in a 2009 conversation, that the virtual appliance sheds its overhead penalty and runs faster in the cloud than it would if it were run unvirtualized in its original corporate data center setting.

The virtual machine has been a concept that's been maturing since the advent of the IBM 360 mainframe in 1964. Now it's 2010, and all that multicore hardware is waiting for something to do. When it's located in big data centers in the cloud, it calls out to smart IT staffs to build (or buy) virtual appliances and send them to it. The cloud makes moving part of the data center workload outside the enterprise a practical alternative.

As we have started to prize energy conservation, reduced cooling needs, and less demand for floor space, IT staffs have thought hard about how to consolidate servers, stack several applications on each server, and split processing responsibilities between their on-premises data center and the highly efficient cloud.

At such an early stage, it's hard to see how all the elements will play out. But it's clear that virtualization changes the ball game in so many ways that new efficiencies are going to emerge, whether the traditionalist data center manager likes it or not. The vague and amorphous term "cloud" is going to quickly evolve toward doing particular computing tasks extremely well. Literally as this is being written, Microsoft is unveiling its Azure cloud, where the task of developing software will shift from being primarily an on-premises function to being an in-the-cloud function, especially when the new software is intended to be deployed there. The gains in efficiency are too great to be ignored.

Microsoft, Oracle, Amazon, and many others will be beneficiaries of the giant step represented by virtualization. But they will always owe a debt to the breakthrough first staged by Mendel Rosenblum and his entrepreneurial wife, Diane, founders of VMware. If they're honest about it, they'll acknowledge that they're standing on the shoulders of giants.

(((**4**)))

JUST OVER
THE HORIZON,
PRIVATE CLOUDS

The adoption of private cloud computing is so young that it's hard to talk about—it's something that doesn't yet exist fully, but is found only in skeletal, experimental form. Many CEOs, CFOs, and COOs are rightly skeptical about how much of their company's most important possession—its data—should take up residence alongside other firms' operations on a shared server. In the multitenant cloud, who knows? Your fiercest competitor might be occupying the same server as you and be grateful for any slop-over of your data.

In this chapter, we'll take a look at why some corporate enterprise data centers, both large and small, will move toward becoming more cloudlike. The users of these internal, or private, clouds, as opposed to the users of the publicly accessible Amazon Elastic Compute Cloud (EC2), Google App Engine, and Microsoft Azure, will not be members of the general public. They will be the employees, business partners, and customers of the business, each of whom will be able to use the internal cloud based on the role he plays in the business.

InformationWeek, which tries to be out front in addressing the interests of business computing professionals, first aired the concept of private clouds as a cover story on April 13, 2009, after hearing about the idea in background interviews over the preceding months. In July, Rackspace announced that it would reserve dedicated servers in its public cloud for those customers seeking to do "private" cloud computing. In August, Amazon Web Services announced that it would offer specially protected facilities within its EC2 public cloud as the Amazon Virtual Private Cloud.

These developments set off a debate inside *InformationWeek* and among cloud proponents and critics throughout the business world. John Foley, editor of the *Plug into the Cloud* feature of www.informationweek.com, asked the question: How can a public cloud supplier suddenly claim to offer private cloud services? Weren't shared, multitenant facilities awkward to redefine as "private"? Some observers think that a public cloud can offer secure private facilities, but any sensible observer (and most CEOs) would agree with Foley's question. How good is a public cloud supplier at protecting "private" operations within its facilities? In fact, there are already some protections in place in the public cloud. There is no slop-over of one customer's data into another's in the multitenant public cloud. If there were, the virtual machines running those operations would experience corrupted instructions and screech to a halt. Still, what if an intruder gains access to the physical server on which your virtual machine is running? Who is responsible if damage is done to the privacy of your customers' identity information through no fault of your company's?

There are no clear answers to these questions yet, although no one assumes that the company that owns the data is somehow absolved of responsibility just because it's moved it into the cloud. What security specialists refer to as the trust boundary, the layer of protections around data that only trusted parties may cross, has moved outside the perimeter of the corporation along with the data, but no one is sure where it has moved to. The question is, what share of responsibility for a lapse in data security would a well-managed cloud data center bear compared to that of the data's owner?

There are good reasons why CEOs don't trust the idea of sending their company's data into the public cloud. For one thing, they are responsible for guaranteeing the privacy and security of the handling of the data. Once it's sent into the cloud, no one inside the company can be completely sure where it's physically located anymore—on which server, which disk array, or maybe even which data center. If something untoward happens at a loosely administered site, it probably will not be an adequate defense to say, "We didn't know our data was *there*." In fact, Greg Shipley, chief technology officer for the Chicago-based information security consultancy Neohapsis, wrote in *Navigating the Storm*, a report by InformationWeek

Analytics, "Cloud computing provides . . . an unsettling level of uncertainty about where our data goes, how it gets there and how protected it will be over time." (See Appendix B.)

Because of these concerns, the security of the cloud is the first question raised in survey after survey whenever business leaders are asked about their plans for cloud computing. And that response is frequently followed by the conclusion that they'd prefer to first implement cloud computing on their own company premises in a "private cloud."

On the face of it, this is an apparent contradiction. By our earlier definition, cloud computing invokes a new business model for distributing external computing power to end users on a pay-as-you-go basis, giving the end user a degree of programmatic control over cloud resources and allowing new economies of scale to assert themselves. At first glance, the idea of achieving competitive economies of scale trips up the notion of a private cloud. With a limited number of users, how will the private cloud achieve the economies of scale that an EC2 or Azure does?

Nevertheless, I think many private enterprises are already seriously considering the private cloud. Until they understand cloud computing from the inside out, these enterprises won't risk data that's critical to the business.

If the on-premises private cloud offers a blend of augmented computing power and also guarantees of data protection, then it is likely to be pressed into service. Its owners will have made a conscious trade-off between guaranteed data security in the cloud and economies of scale. A private cloud doesn't have to compete with EC2 or Azure to justify its existence. It merely needs to be cheaper than the architecture in the data center that preceded it. If it is, the private cloud's advocates will have a firm business case for building it out. We'll discuss security further in Chapter 6.

Hardware Choices for the Private Cloud

Part of the argument for adopting public cloud computing is that companies pay only for what they use, without an up-front outlay in capital expense. But that argument can also be turned on its head and used for the private cloud. An IT manager could say, "We're making the capital investment anyway. We have 100 servers that will need a hardware refresh later this year. Why not use this purchase as the first step toward converting our data center into something resembling those external clouds?" The benefits of private clouds will flow out of such decision making.

Google is building its own servers because the configurations of servers in the marketplace so far do not meet the cost/benefit requirements of its cloud architecture. If Google, Yahoo!, and others continue to publish information on their data centers, the data center managers at companies will figure out how to approximate a similar hardware makeup. Indeed, Dell is rapidly shifting gears from being a personal computing and business computing supplier to becoming a cloud supplier as well. As I was working on a report at the 2009 Cloud Computing Conference & Expo, Barton George, Dell's newly appointed cloud computing evangelist, poked his head through the door to tell me that Dell is in the process of discovering the best designs for cloud servers to produce for private cloud builders.

Dell's staff is practiced at managing the construction and delivery of personal computers and business servers. Why not turn those skills toward becoming a cloud hardware supplier? In doing so, it will be turning a cherished business practice upside down. Dell lets a buyer self-configure the computer she wants on the Dell Web site. Then, Dell builds and delivers that computer in a highly competitive way. To become a cloud supplier, it will have to figure out in advance what makes a good cloud server, concentrate on getting the best deals on parts for those types of servers, and then, upon a customer order, quickly deliver thousands of identical units. Forrest Norrod, general manager of Dell's Data Center Solutions, said his business unit has supplied enough types of servers to Amazon, Microsoft Azure, and other cloud data centers to have derived a handful of types that are favored by cloud builders.

Cisco Systems, a new entrant in the blade server market, is a primary supplier to the NASA Nebula cloud under construction in Mountain View, California, and would doubtless like to see its highly virtualizable Unified Computing System used to build additional clouds.

HP and IBM plan to do so as well, although IBM's deepest wish is to find a new mass market into which to sell its own Power processor, not the rival x86 servers built by Intel and AMD that currently dominate public cloud construction. Whether IBM will be able to convince customers to use its processor remains to be seen, but it has succeeded in the past at extending its product lines into successive technology evolutions of business. At the very least, expect the Power processors to appear in a Big Blue version of the public cloud still to come. Sun Microsystems also would like to see its hardware incorporated into cloud data centers, but its UltraSPARC server line is now owned by Oracle. The uncertainty associated with that acquisition will temporarily stall cloud construction with UltraSPARC parts. Nevertheless, it's imminent that "cloud"-flavored servers will find their way into mainstream catalogs and well-known distribution channels, such as those of Dell, HP, Cisco Systems, and IBM.

It remains unlikely that CIOs and IT managers will start building a private cloud as a tentative or experimental project inside the company; few have the capital to waste on half measures. Instead, as the idea of cloud computing takes hold, small, medium-sized, and large enterprises will start recasting their data centers as cloud clusters. The example of public clouds and the economies of scale that flow from them will prove compelling.

This doesn't mean that stalwart Unix servers and IBM mainframes will be pushed onto a forklift and carted away, replaced by sets of, say, $2,400 x86 servers. On the contrary, proprietary Unix servers and mainframes run many business applications that can't be easily converted to the x86 instruction set. For many years to come, applications in COBOL, FORTRAN, RPG, Smalltalk, and other languages, written in-house years ago or customized from what is often a product no longer in existence, will still be running in the corporate data center. But there are some applications running on legacy systems that can be converted to the x86 architecture and run in the internal cloud, and many new applications will assume the x86 architecture is their presumed target. Private clouds may never achieve the economies of scale of the big public clouds, but they don't have to. They only need to be cheaper to operate than legacy systems.

The process is already well under way. While Unix and the mainframe remain a presence, the fastest-growing operating systems in corporate data centers are Windows Server and Linux, both designed for x86 systems. The trend to consolidate more applications on one server through virtualization, thereby reducing the total number of servers, can be done on any of the named architectures, but the most vigorous activity is virtualization of x86 servers. VMware, the market leader, grew from a start-up to $2 billion in revenues in 10 years. VMware, Citrix Systems, and now Microsoft produce virtualization products for the x86 servers, with open source products Xen and KVM available as well. It's possible to cluster such machines together and run them as a pooled resource from one management console, a first step toward the private cloud.

The Steps Leading to the Private Cloud

But why would a company want to build its own private cloud? Like the public cloud, the private cloud would be built out of cost-effective PC parts. It would be run as a pool of servers functioning something like a single giant computer through a layer of virtual machine management software. Workloads can be spread around the pool so that the load is balanced across the available servers. If more capacity is needed for a particular workload, the private cloud, like the public cloud, would be elastic. The workload can be moved to where that capacity already exists, or more hardware can be brought on line to add capacity. After disposing of peak loads, any server that isn't needed can be shut down to save energy.

Furthermore, the end users of the private cloud can self-provision themselves with any kind of computer—a virtual machine to run in the cloud—that they wish. The private cloud can measure their use of the virtual machine and bill their department for hours of use based on the operating costs for the type of system they chose. This self-provisioning and chargeback system is already available through the major virtualization software vendors as what's called a "lab manager." That product was aimed at a group of users who are likely to be keenly interested in self-provisioning—the software developers who need different types of software environments in which to test-drive their code. After they know that their code will run as intended, they turn it over to a second group of potential private cloud users, the quality assurance managers. These managers want to test the code for the load it can carry—how many concurrent users, how many transactions at one time? They want to make sure that it does the work intended and will work with other pieces of software that must depend on its output.

Software development, testing, and quality assurance is a major expense in most companies' IT budget. If the private cloud can have an impact on that expense, then there is an economic justification to support its implementation. But beyond the software professionals, there are many other potential internal users of this new resource. Frequently, line managers and business analysts, who understand the transactions and business processes that drive the company, lack the means of analyzing those processes from the data that they produce. If they had that analysis on a rapid basis for time periods that they chose to define, such as a surge in a seasonal product, then they would be able to design new business processes and services based on the results.

By giving priority to such work, the private cloud could apportion resources in a more elastic manner than its predecessor data center filled with legacy systems. The many separate parts of the traditional data center had their own work to do; few were available for reassignment on a temporary basis. Or the private cloud could monitor the company's Web site, and when it's in danger of being overloaded, assign more resources to it rather than lose potential customers through turned-away or timed-out visitors.

Once a portion of the data center has been "pooled" and starts to be managed in a cloudlike manner, its example may bring more advocates to the fore, arguing that they too should have access to cloud-style resources. It might sound as if the private cloud is a prospect that remains far off in the future, but virtualization of the data center, as noted in the previous chapter, is already well under way. Such virtualization lays the groundwork for the move to a private cloud.

As cloud computing grows in importance in the economy, top management will ask if it is possible to achieve internally the economies that they're reading about in public clouds. Those that have built up skills in x86 servers and built out pools of virtualized servers will be able to answer yes, it is.

The next step would be to acquire the layer of virtualization management software to overlay the pool, provide monitoring and management tools, and give yourself automated ways of load balancing and migrating virtual machines around.

VMware is leading the field with its vSphere 4 infrastructure package and vCenter management tools. In fact, vCenter can provide a view of the virtualized servers as a pooled resource, as if they were one giant computer, and manage them as a unit, although there is a limit to the number of physical servers one vCenter management console can cover. Citrix Systems' XenSource unit, the Virtual Iron part of Oracle, and Microsoft's System Center Virtual Machine Manager product can do many of these things as well.

A manager using vSphere 4 and vCenter can track what virtual machines are running, what jobs they're doing, and the percentage of their host server that is fully utilized. By moving virtual machines around from physical server to physical server, the data center manager can balance the workload, move virtual machines to servers that have spare capacity, and shut down servers that aren't needed to save energy.

Moving to a private cloud may not necessarily be a goal at many business data centers. But many of the fundamental trends driving efficient computing will point them in that direction anyway. Those who have built out an x86 data center and organized it as a virtualized pool will be well positioned to complete the migration to a private cloud. The better the economics of the cloud portion of the data center look internally, the more likely it is that the rest of the data center will be converted into the private cloud.

There's a second set of economics pushing the corporate data center toward a private cloud as well. Whether the CEO, the CFO, or the CIO likes it or not, there is going to be an explosion of computer power and sophisticated services on the Web, both in large public clouds and among smaller entrepreneurial providers of services that run in the public cloud. They will have much in common in that they will follow the standards of Web services, distribute their wares over the Internet, and keep their cost of operation as low as possible.

Even if top management in enterprises can live with higher costs in its own data centers, and there are good data security reasons for why it will, that still leaves the problem of coordinating everything that could be done for the company by new and increasingly specialized business services in the external cloud.

Such services already exist, but they remain at an early stage of development compared to their potential. If you're dealing with a new customer and he places a large order with your firm, your order capture system goes out on the Web and checks his credit rating before you begin to process the order. If a $500,000 order comes in from a recognized customer in good standing, but the address is different from the one you normally ship to, the order fulfillment system automatically goes out on the Web, enlists an address checking system to see whether the customer has a facility at the address listed, and collects data on whether the customer might expect the type of goods ordered shipped to that location. These services save businesses valuable time and labor by performing automatically things that would take well-paid staff members hours of labor to perform. Another example is online freight handling services, which can now take your order to ship goods between two points; consult their own directories of carriers, tolls, and current energy prices; and deliver a quote in seconds that proves valid, no matter where in the country you're seeking to make a delivery. They will find the lowest-cost carrier with the attributes that you're seeking—shipment tracking, confirmed delivery, reliable on-time delivery—in a manner that surpasses what your company's shipping department could do with its years of experience.

On every front, online information systems are dealing with masses of information to yield competitive results. To ignore such services is to put your business in peril, and indeed few businesses are ignoring them. The next generation may cede key elements of programmatic control to customers, allowing them to plug in more variables, change the destination of an order en route, fulfill other special requirements, and invoke partnerships and business relationships that work for them, ratcheting up the value of such services.

The alignment of the internal data center with external resources will become an increasingly important competitive factor, and many managers already sense it.

They've also seen a precedent. At one time, corporations built out high-performance proprietary networks to link headquarters to manufacturing and divisions at different locations.

Two of these networks, Digital Equipment's DECnet and IBM's Systems Network Architecture (SNA), looked like solid investments for many years. But the growth of the Internet, at first a phenomenon that the corporation could ignore, began to take on a new meaning. The Internet could handle e-mail and file transfer for any company that was equipped to send things over a Transmission Control Protocol/Internet Protocol (TCP/IP) network. As the Internet became the default connection between universities, government agencies, and some companies, the cost of not having a TCP/IP network internally went up and up. At the same time, a vigorous debate ensued over whether TCP/IP was good enough for the needs of the modern enterprise beyond e-mail.

As previously mentioned, TCP/IP, the protocol on which the Internet is based, had been designed to survive a nuclear attack. It was a network of networks. If a segment of the network were to go down, the other segments would automatically route around it. It made for what critics labeled a "chatty" protocol. A router would map a good route for a particular message, then call up the next router on that route. "Are you there?" it would ask, and it would get a ping back, "Yes, I'm up and running." The sender would ping again, "Are you ready?" and the router on the next leg of the route would answer, "Yes, I'm ready." The message would be sent. The sender would then ask, "Did you receive the message?" and would get back a response of either "Yes, I did," or "No, send again."

Neither DECnet nor IBM's SNA would have tolerated such chitchat. It wasn't efficient, according to their designers. And perhaps TCP/IP is a bit of a Chatty Kathy or Gabby Hayes. But what made it hard to resist was the fact that it worked in so many cases. It was sufficient for much enterprise networking, which was discovered as enterprises started relying on internal TCP/IP networks called intranets to carry traffic derived from the Internet. These intranets turned out to be "good enough" even when their performance lagged that of the proprietary networks. And the messages got through with high reliability. They might on rare occasions arrive minutes or even hours later than the sender intended, when a router outage led to concentrations of traffic on the nearby routers drafted by many other routers as the way around the outage. Instead of maintaining an expensive proprietary network across the country, the company could let its internal TCP/IP network originate the message, then let the Internet serve as its external connection to other facilities, partners, suppliers, and customers.

If there was still resistance to conversion, it faded at the mention of the price. The Internet was free, and the TCP/IP protocol used inside the company was freely available, built into various versions of Unix and Linux and even Microsoft's Windows Server. When internal operation is aligned with the external world operations—and the cost is the lowest available—the decision on what to do next becomes inevitable. A similar alignment will occur between external cloud data centers and the internal cloud.

To prepare for that day, it's important to start expanding x86 administration skills and x86 virtualization skills rather than sitting out this early phase of cloud computing. There are immediate benefits to starting to reorient your computing infrastructure around the concept of the private cloud. This is an evolutionary, not revolutionary, process that will occur over many years.

I can hear the voices saying, don't go down the route of the private cloud: it will destroy your security mechanisms; it will drag down your performance in your most trusted systems; it will lead to disarray. I think instead that those who can't move in this direction will find that they are increasingly at a competitive disadvantage. Whether you're ready for it or not, cloud computing is coming to the rest of the world, and those who don't know how to adapt are going to find themselves in the path of those who do and who are getting stronger.

The private data center will remain private, that necessary place of isolation from the outside world where data is safe and someone always knows where it is. The private cloud in that data center is as much behind the firewall and able to implement defenses in depth as any other part of the data center.

The day will come when the virtual machines running on x86 servers will have a defensive watchman guarding the hypervisor, that new layer of software that is so close to all the operations of the server. The watchman will know the patterns of the server and will be looking for the specific things an intruder might do that would vary those patterns, blowing the whistle at the first untoward movement that it spots. In response, an automated manager will halt the virtual machine's processing, register what point it was at with the business logic and the data, then erase the virtual machine. A new virtual machine will then be constructed and loaded with the application instructions and data and pick up where its predecessor left off.

If the intruder is still out there, he may find a way to insinuate himself again, but the watchman will be ready. The more extreme advocates of security say that this process can be pushed to a more logical conclusion, where the virtual machine is arbitrarily stopped, killed, and deleted from the system every 30 minutes, whether it needs to be or not. A new one spun up from a constantly checked master on a secure server will be a known, clean entity. Such a practice would make it so discouraging for a skilled hacker—who needs, say, 29.5 minutes to steal an ID, find a password, await authentication, and then try to figure out a position from which to steal data—that it would be a level of defense in depth that exceeds those devised before. Such a watchman is just starting to appear from start-up network security vendors; the hypervisor firewall with intruder detection already exists as a leading-edge product. Only the periodic kill-off mechanism still needs to be built into virtual machine management.

As the desire for private clouds builds, the technology convergence that has produced cloud computing will be given new management tools and new security tools to perfect its workings. We are at the beginning of that stage, not its end. Guaranteeing the secure operation of virtual machines running in the private enterprise data center—and in the public cloud—will enable the two sites to coordinate their operations. And that's ultimately what the private cloud leads to: a federated operation of private and public sites that further enhances the economies of scale captured in cloud computing.

THE HYBRID CLOUD

It may seem unlikely to some observers that this will ever come to pass, but behind the vision for a private cloud is the tantalizing prospect that it might one day be coordinated with the public cloud. Those big data centers on the Internet could be used as backup for and absorbers of the peak workloads of the traditional data center.

If this did come about, the relationship between the public and the private cloud would be focused on managing the spikes in demand that occur in every business: accounting's close of a quarter; the launch of a new product; the onslaught of customers during the holiday shopping season. For much of the year, a company's computers have a predictable load that runs far below these peaks. But since they know that the spike is coming, computer professionals have learned to oversupply the data center with servers, network capacity, and disks. The need for surplus capacity is so taken for granted that it is rarely questioned as an IT manager proceeds to supply it. Not doing so would be more likely to raise eyebrows.

In a world of increasing operations costs, increasing energy costs, and rising global temperatures, such an approach may no longer be viable. Businesses frequently take it upon themselves to operate in both a cost-effective and a responsible manner. Hybrid cloud computing, where the private cloud shakes hands with the hyperefficient public cloud, will be the new way to do so.

Before getting to such a solution, however, every business is going to have to confront a set of well-entrenched problems. Anyone who has ever been responsible for some part of his company's computing knows the constant tension between the need to maintain operations and the desire to put more resources into software applications and equipment to support new products and services.

Reduced Overhead, Steady-State Operation

When I joined *Computerworld* in 1984, a constant topic in the news was the so-called application backlog, the long list of software needed by businesses that wasn't getting written. The in-house developers charged with producing new applications were usually behind on the deadlines set for the current projects. They were frequently called away from development efforts to troubleshoot problems that kept popping up in the software that was already in use. Just keeping the place running, sometimes referred to as "maintenance," sapped everybody's time and consumed the lion's share of the company's computing budget.

We may be on the eve of a brave new world of cloud computing, but in some respects, not all that much has changed. Gartner Inc. says that 75 percent of the information technology budget still goes to maintenance and only 25 percent to new projects and initiatives. For years, everyone has wanted to reverse those numbers. But two severe recessions in this first decade of the twenty-first century have made companies leery of overstaffing and overspending on IT development. Everybody is trying to do more with less. The application backlog, which today looks more like a service backlog or a business process backlog, continues undiminished. Frustration mounts.

Soon after I went to work for *Information Week*, the question arose, why was the maintenance burden so heavy? Why did the needle never move off the 75 percent mark on the gauge (an average across many businesses) year after year? The answer in part was the ongoing complexity of corporate data centers. In many cases, the venerable IBM mainframe sits at the core, with powerful Unix boxes running database systems and important legacy applications. The corporate Web site is being run on a set of Linux boxes, and many employees are tied into Windows servers for Office and other desktop applications.

In fact, most corporate data centers have one of just about everything. In one corner, a legacy HP server is running its old proprietary operating system; in another, an ancient Digital Equipment Corp. server is running a different operating system. Even though DEC disappeared inside Compaq Computer years ago (and Compaq, in turn, inside HP), these old products grind on. There are still some of all these machines around—and their legacy applications won't coordinate very well with the cloud. Even new software, bought as packages from Oracle, SAP, or Microsoft, tends to get customized by its new owner and set up with special dependencies on other systems. As the complexity grows, so does the work of the computing professionals who tend these systems and keep everything on track.

Most of all, they have to guard against occasional peaks in workload that may prove to be too much for any one system, resulting in a crash. If a key data center system fails, then other systems that depend on it will stall, as their calls for computing results will go unanswered. Because the professionals managing this complexity are responsible for keeping everything running, they've learned to overallocate resources rather than trying to cut the margin too thin. For many years, a single x86 server would run one application to avoid the possibility of hidden conflicts between two different applications on the same server. Such a practice was wasteful of hardware; it often used only 15 percent of the server's capabilities, and this figure sometimes dropped into the 5 to 7 percent range, but the solution was cheap compared to the pain of user protests over outages and the expense to fix them. Likewise, disk drives allocated to an application for storing its data were also oversupplied; a typical rate of disk drive usage to this day is only 30 percent—excess capital expense that might be avoided through a different method of managing these resources.

Much of the impetus behind the current drive to implement virtualized servers in data centers is the desire to address these problems. On a virtualized host, as many as six or eight applications can be run at the same time without being in danger of encroaching on one another. A hypervisor supervises the virtual machine traffic and enforces boundaries between the applications. Through virtualization, server utilization jumps from 15 percent to 66 to 70 percent; some margin of headroom still needs to be maintained so that bursts of activity in one or more applications can be accommodated. The initial drive into virtualization has yielded big rewards in reducing the number of servers needed in a crowded data center. It has reduced electricity consumption and, in some cases, simplified application management, although realistically, another element of complexity has been introduced into the data center as well.

A glimmer of hope can be found in this virtualized section of the data center. First of all, there are radically fewer server architectures in it. Instead of Sun UltraSPARC, DEC Alpha, and IBM POWER or mainframe microprocessors, the data center is constructed from a single set of x86 microprocessors, such as Intel's Xeon. The new data center design might resemble the way Google builds its thousands of cloud servers, or perhaps reflect a cloud design offered by Dell. This virtualized server set is run as a pooled resource, viewed constantly through a single management console that can balance loads, shift virtual machines around, and even add new hardware to the cluster without interrupting any business operations. In short, it's being managed much like a cloud server cluster.

The next step in the evolution of this data center is for an ambitious CIO or IT manager to set a goal of utilizing the server cluster at a rate closer to 100 percent. Furthermore, he thinks he knows how to do that: get close to the typical level of total use. That is, the internal cloud will run at what amounts to the data center's average or steady state of operation, which can be culled from server logs and management system views. To implement such an approach would result in major hardware savings, if a method of offloading the peaks of activity above steady state that will still occur can be found. No one will actually shoot to operate at 100 percent utilization of servers all the time, but 90 percent might be reasonable if there were good coordination between this private cloud on the enterprise's premises and a public cloud on the Internet.

It's this hybrid of private, on-premises clouds and public clouds—the potential for offloading work during peak activity—that highlights cloud computing's potential value to businesses. The offloading of peaks has even been given a name: these shifted workloads are called "cloudbursts." Such an approach could conceivably work for business users of many kinds. The traditional data center could streamline its operations, offloading peaks as a minimal invocation of the public cloud. Small or large businesses might find ways to use the cloud on a more regular basis and avoid building out a data center that tends to get more and more complex in the first place. Let the cloud managers manage complexity. That's what they're good at. The business can then just pay for what it uses, rather than repeatedly overspending on hardware.

Isn't this just wishful thinking? What about CEOs' concerns about customer data traveling out to the public cloud, where the IT managers lose track of it? Don't spikes in activity include customer data?

Yes, spikes in workloads often include sensitive data. So an IT manager needs to analyze what work is appropriate to send out to the cloud and what is not. He doesn't need to send the work that is causing the spike, if the data should stay in house. Because the virtualized servers are being managed as a pool, if the operations manager offloads some equivalent to the spike, he'll pick up the capacity he needs to continue operating. This is a fresh subject for computer professionals in enterprise IT, but they're already identifying several types of workload that could be shipped off to the cloud without posing much of a threat to secure company operations.

The first such type of workload is software testing. Hardly anyone in her right mind wants to steal unfinished, unproven software designed for some purpose specific to a single given company. The testing of the software in cloud environments would involve intensive use of many servers for short periods of time, almost a definition of the kind of job that the cloud is good at. In addition, quality assurance of new software is a closely related job that could be performed in the cloud.

The staging of new applications, where they're configured to run with all the other pieces of software that they depend on, is a third transferable job. A new human resource management or new accounting application is first launched in a staged environment to see if anything goes wrong. If it does, that environment has been kept separate from the business's data center production systems, which must be protected from interruption at all times.

So if an IT manager is already operating a virtualized environment, can he just ship his virtual machines off to the cloud to run there? In a few scenarios this would work, but today the handshake is harder to execute than that. One of the most commonly used clouds is Amazon's Elastic Compute Cloud (EC2), but it runs virtual machines in a proprietary virtualized file format called Amazon Machine Images (AMI). Amazon wants you to package up your workload in its proprietary AMI, not in a more common format that you may already be working with internally, and send it to EC2 ready to go. So this handshake idea between clouds still involves some coordination steps.

One company, rPath, that automates the building of virtualized workloads can package your application and operating system as an AMI and send it to EC2 through its free downloadable tool, rBuilder. Elastra and RightScale can also handle the task. Other companies are sure to supply the same service soon. You can also do it yourself with the tools that Amazon makes available at its Amazon Web Services site.

There are additional ways to build out a private infrastructure as if it were designed to work with a public cloud. If you build applications equipped with the Eucalyptus Systems application programming interfaces to run in your private cloud, they will work on premises in the same manner as they would if they were sent off premises to EC2. They will load into servers and run on cue, invoking temporary storage or permanent storage in your private cloud in a way that's identical to EC2's. Using the same APIs as EC2 leads to equipping the private cloud with the same services found in the external cloud. When the time comes to split the workloads between the two, it's less of a coordination headache. Part of the workload can be shipped off and run on its EC2 destination server the same as if it were still on premises. So far, Eucalyptus supports a subset of the EC2 services, including loading a virtual machine onto a server, enlisting Elastic Block Store for temporarily storing the application and its data, and tapping Simple Storage Service, also known as S3, for long-term storage.

Eucalyptus is an open source project that grew out of the University of California at Santa Barbara's computer science department under Professor Rich Wolski. It developed cloud interfaces that closely mimic those provided by EC2. Amazon Web Services regards its cloud APIs as proprietary, which prevents other cloud suppliers from using them, but it appears to have no objection to those who choose to use Eucalyptus's open source APIs. Amazon would like to see the EC2's APIs become as widely accepted as possible and has not challenged or interfered with the operation of Eucalyptus's APIs. If enterprises build private clouds using Eucalyptus, these operations will be highly compatible with EC2, a development that Amazon favors. Wolski, now CTO of the firm Eucalyptus Systems, a company that he cofounded to build products around the Eucalyptus APIs and expand them, says that he is highly confident of Eucalyptus's ability to maintain ongoing compatibility with EC2.

In September 2009, Eucalyptus Systems provided what's likely to be another widely used building block of the private cloud. Eucalyptus Enterprise Edition can provide APIs for cloud services being built in VMware virtualized environments, the type most frequently found in private enterprises. In the past, there was a wall between VMware's virtual machines and EC2's AMI format, since the two formats did not build virtual machines in the same way with the same functions and were incompatible. The Enterprise Edition software, however, invokes a converter that changes VMware's virtual machine into an AMI recognized by EC2. Therefore, a workload in the VMware private cloud can now migrate across the boundary that used to separate it from the Amazon cloud. This opens up another path for coordination between public and private clouds. Eucalyptus Enterprise Edition is a commercial product rather than open source code, with a charge for each processor on which it runs.

At this point, Eucalyptus has stopped short of trying to create look-alike APIs for some of Amazon's more advanced services, such as the SimpleDB database service, Amazon Elastic MapReduce, or Amazon Relational Database Service. Nevertheless, Eucalyptus has broken down several barriers to constructing the private cloud. Its core Eucalyptus APIs are in the public arena as open source code and are likely to be invoked by more companies seeking to create a private cloud that aligns with a public one.

A related effort is Simple API for Cloud Application Services, another open source project led by Zend Technologies. It seeks to provide an API for types of service that are found in the public cloud, then let different clouds support that API if they so choose. Simple API's aim is to allow an application running in an enterprise to invoke, say, a Simple API for storage and receive the storage service available from the cloud it's dealing with—if that cloud supports Simple API. That may be a big if. On the other hand, Simple API may catch on as a way to level the playing field and give newcomers a shot at attracting business from emerging private clouds. Simple API already works across the Nirvanix Storage Delivery Network, a public cloud storage provider, and Amazon's S3. Nirvanix supports Simple API for storage. Amazon doesn't, but S3 is accessible anyway, because the Eucalyptus API for S3 is publicly available.

It's still very early in the game, but these open source and commercial initiatives show how private clouds may soon be built and find the means to synchronize their operations with public clouds. Commercial products probably aren't far behind the open source examples. In some cases, front-end management services, such as Skytap and RightScale, already accept and manage an enterprise's virtual workloads for the cloud, even if they are generated by different hypervisors. They or companies like them may extend that ability and start navigating the manmade barriers between private cloud operations and the public cloud.

Coming, an Explosion of Cloud Services

I'd like to cite one more development that makes me optimistic about that possibility. VMware knows that Amazon's EC2 is the most popular cloud infrastructure and that Amazon is seeking to convert the world to its own, not VMware's, virtual machine file format. VMware, in turn, is seeking to start up more cloud suppliers that can support its Virtual Machine Disk format (VMDK) files. VMware is trying to seed public cloud services by providing prospective cloud vendors with vCloud Express, a set of tools for allowing a new cloud service to set up customer self-provisioning, pay-as-you-go cloud services that run VMware virtual machines. VMware knows that it will have an advantage over Amazon Web Services if it can get cloud suppliers to do this, as IT managers are already using its products in their data centers.

"This notion of federation—getting the internal and external resources to work together—we think that's a differentiator for VMware," said VMware CEO Paul Maritz at his firm's user conference, VMworld, in September 2009. *Information-Week* added its own analysis:

> Although Maritz didn't say so at the San Francisco event, vCloud express is a counterstroke to the popular, easily available Amazon EC2 cloud services. Amazon relies on the open source Xen hypervisor to run workloads in its cloud, not VMware's product set. As a result EC2's Amazon Machine Image requires VMware customers to recast their virtual machines in Amazon's AMI.

VMware is trying to capitalize on the incompatibility. It is aiming to help competing cloud service providers to make headway against Amazon based on an ease of use feature.

There are existing suppliers that want to grow their cloud businesses that are eager to take VMware up on its offer. Executives from Terremark, an online data center supplier of managed hosts, said on September 2, 2009 that it had implemented vCloud Express at its facilities and would offer cloud services through it, as had RightScale. In addition, executives from Verizon Business, the business computing unit of the Verizon wireless company, and AT&T said that they plan to offer vCloud Express–type services but would add to their entry-level nature with more sophisticated offerings. Verizon's Computing as a Service cloud offering has run VMware virtual machines since June. Savvis, a supplier of co-location services in which data center servers tied directly to the Internet may be leased, says it plans to do the same with VMware virtual machines and the VMDK file format.

Where there's this much activity, a rapid expansion of cloud services is clearly about to occur. So the idea of building the private cloud and having it hand off spikes in its workload to the public cloud may not be so far-fetched after all. If data centers can be built accurately to a steady-state operation, without having to worry about occasional spikes, this would diminish or eliminate the compulsive overprovisioning that's been going on for three decades. This would give the computer professionals a chance to pour more resources into new software and new services for the business and fewer resources into maintenance.

The Buzz Is Back

At various stages in the rapid expansion of computing, a certain buzz has been evident at gatherings where people are so excited that they can't stop talking about how awesome the latest technology is. They assure each other that they are committed to doing something with it. I remember hearing that buzz before the introduction of the IBM PC, after the announcement of the Apple Macintosh, and when Java appeared as the seemingly ideal language for the rapidly emerging Internet computing space. I heard it again at the Cloud Computing Conference & Expo in Santa Clara, California, in November 2009.

During the recession of 2008–2009, computer shows were forlorn places, with the number of salespeople staffing booths sometimes exceeding that of attendees wandering the aisles. And they were unnaturally subdued. At the cloud conference, a break in the stage proceedings led to attendees congregating on the exhibit show floor. They were talking about Amazon's latest expansion of service; they were talking about Rackspace and Savvis claiming that they could offer private cloud services in their shared facilities. Could they really do that? They were talking about the vast new services that would be invented in the cloud—the next Facebook, the next big thing that would attract 350 million users in no time at all.

It was the excited buzz of certainty that something big was afoot and that they were going to be part of it.

Part of that certainty was a growing understanding that a new resource has come into being that enables new computing services and new alignments among computing services. The hybrid cloud looks like one of those beneficial alignments, still a few years off from its ultimate fulfillment, but coming just the same and opening up a new expansive round of possibilities that businesses must embrace and act upon if they want to stay competitive.

$(((\mathbf{6})))$

OVERCOMING
RESISTANCE
TO THE CLOUD

It sounds simple. Corporate data centers will align themselves with the public cloud and realize heretofore unattainable economies of scale from this new and accessible form of Internet computing. But it's not that simple. There are too many vested interests that are ready to place obstacles in the path of a smooth and common-standards-based migration to the cloud and between clouds.

If hybrid cloud computing is to become the data center of the future, as we concluded that it would in Chapter 5, it will be necessary for computer operations managers to be able to move workloads freely between their corporate data centers and a public cloud.

This movement between internal and external centers will need to occur in ways that minimize friction between the two. What we have today instead is friction and resistance to the notion of cloud computing at so many levels of the process that it's still hard to conceive of doing this on any sustained basis. Several technical barriers exist, but we can start with dislike for the term *cloud computing* on the part of the CEO and other top-level executives, incompatible file formats demanded by the different virtualization vendors, and proprietary moves by cloud service suppliers. But skillful users, an increasing number of standards, and a growing supply of open source code are keeping pressure on the artificial constraints, and some of them will soon fall away.

What's in a Name? CEO Opposition

Let's start at the top. As Bob Evans of *InformationWeek* reported, when HP CEO Mark Hurd, as no-nonsense a personality as they come, spoke to a group of CEOs in late 2009, he described the future possibilities of computing using the term *cloud* and was nearly jeered off the stage. "Here I am talking about the cloud and all kinds of cool things that can happen with the cloud, and I got a lot of boos, um, after that. It started with the whole term, 'cloud.'"

After that experience, Hurd stated that "cloud computing" was an inadequate phrase for the things he wanted to talk about. In a rare moment of harmony for two competitors, IBM's CEO Sam Palmisano agreed, saying that *cloud* was "an unfortunate name" and suggested "highly virtualized infrastructure" instead. That phrase misses the mark when it comes to the self-service, end user empowerment, and multitenant nature of most cloud computing.

Leaving aside Palmisano's proposed renaming, when you are looking for opposition to the term *cloud*, you don't need to look far. It's possible that Larry Ellison's outspoken jibes have resonated with those who find the term confusing, misapplied, or misleading. Soon Oracle will be directly involved in cloud computing, as its second-tier executives well know, and perhaps Ellison will then clarify his remarks for the benefit of CEOs everywhere. In the meantime, opposition will continue to come from those who can't take the time to wrestle with the implications of what it means.

Admittedly, "cloud" can be an awkward term to explain. It has evolved as a descriptive term that captures a new computing distribution pattern and business model, at a time when that pattern is still getting established. Most likely, "the cloud" will rapidly evolve into more specific forms of computing that reflect what particular clouds will do. These clouds will take on more specific names, reflecting a concrete form of computer service.

An example of a cloud with a more specific definition might be an IBM cloud, which will almost certainly include a combination of x86 instruction set servers, proprietary IBM servers, and perhaps IBM mainframe clusters. This will be a "heterogeneous cloud" that is capable of hosting a wide variety of workloads, or possibly a "legacy system cloud" that is capable of running old Unix and mainframe workloads as well as new Linux and Windows systems. Amazon can't do that, so a large number of enterprises that are interested in cloud computing will have reason to look to IBM or elsewhere. Such a data center will sacrifice some simplicity of management and economies of scale in order to be able to host a variety of data center applications. So far, IBM hasn't drawn a road map of how its cloud facilities will be architected, although it offers some specific products that would lend themselves to private internal cloud operations.

For the moment, we're left with the generic term *cloud computing*, whether Mark Hurd's audiences like it or not. It captures the notion of a widely available, low-cost service that is available on the Internet, which is the ultimate network "cloud."

Data and Identity Security at Stake

In addition to etymological opposition, resistance on additional grounds may come from CEOs, chief security officers, chief information officers, and/or database administrators, all of whom will want to know how it's possible to send the company's most valuable asset, its data, outside the firewall.

The answers will emerge over the next two years as the largest vendors and innovative start-ups tackle the problem. In many cases, instead of solving the problem in its own labs, one of the established vendors will buy a start-up with a piece of technology that resolves some additional piece of the puzzle.

Secure ways can be established to move sensitive data between the enterprise and a public cloud and handle it safely once it is there. But early cloud computing initiatives have not progressed to the point where they can do so and keep the data owner in compliance with all regulations, such as the PCI regulations that govern retail transaction data. As we've discussed, Amazon has announced that it will host "private" cloud computing within its public cloud infrastructure by imposing the use of a virtual private network—encrypted data moving over the public network—and other restrictions on how it deals with the "private" processing part of its business. This is not enough to meet businesses' objections to sending customer identity, health, or financial data outside the company, but it's a start. In the long run, if secure procedures are established and are proved to meet or exceed enterprise regulations, then the requirements may be changed to match the new conditions created by cloud computing. But revising regulations is a slow process. It will take established players—bankers, insurance professionals, equity traders—several years of illustrating the security of unregulated data exchange via cloud computing and lobbying for a review on regulated data to open the door to change.

After data management comes the ticklish issue of user identity as users migrate back and forth between applications in the enterprise and in the cloud. Already, Microsoft, Salesforce.com, and others say that they can provide a "federated identity"—a procedure by which one identity management system handles the requirements for user identity for several different applications. The "federated" identity moves with the end user as she changes applications so that she doesn't have to supply multiple user names and passwords. In effect, she logs in once and gets access to all the applications that she needs without having to do so again, regardless of whether the applications are in the enterprise or in the cloud. Microsoft says that it can do more than just enforce controls on end users as they cross the company boundary and move out into its Azure cloud. It can identify and authenticate users from other companies or from the public at large. It can use identity management from multiple directories, in addition to its own Active Directory, and use multiple types of identity confirmation. Its Identity Platform serves as a metadirectory for end user access control. Microsoft's approach allows the application to demand a certain kind of unique identifier, a digital certificate, an Active Directory name and title, or a Windows token. The system retrieves that identifier, if it's available, and submits it to the application, which accepts or rejects it. Identity under this system is "claims based," or just a claimed identifier until the application accepts it. Some firms, such as start-up Symplified in Boulder, Colorado, say that they can also federate identity between enterprise and cloud users, relying on directory sources.

As this was being written, Fujitsu senior director Daniel Lawson said that in early 2010, his firm will launch cloud processing services at its Dallas, Texas, and Sunnyvale, California, data centers. The Dallas center will be secure enough to meet the PCI regulations. Fujitsu can do this by implementing secure FTP setups that ensure that the data that is sent arrives at its destination intact and unchanged and is handled by secure processes afterward. That is, a process that might have been used by a financial institution to move data from one business unit to another has now been extended to the cloud.

Fujitsu goes a step further and says that it is planning ways to be able to handle Health Insurance Portability and Accountability Act (HIPAA) data, which includes patient health-care information. The privacy standards involved will make HIPAA a steep requirement to meet in the cloud environment, and such a development may still be years off. Fujitsu's Lawson acknowledges that not all health-care processing may be suitable for the cloud, but he believes that some of it can be executed there.

Unisys has also announced that it will provide services to support corporate cloud operations and is betting that its ability to deliver a more secure environment will give it a share of future cloud activity. Savvis, Verizon Business, and AT&T plan to offer VMware-based cloud services that go beyond the elementary controls contained in VMware's vCloud Express software. One area that they will emphasize is greater security of operations.

Avoiding Lock-In

Cloud advocates will then encounter their final barrier, vendor lock-in. Early cloud users will have to navigate the usual attempts by vendors to establish proprietary control in bids for industry dominance. This vendor play for dominance has been a prominent feature of each previous phase of computing. Vendors have a right to seek a return on their investment. But I find it hard to believe that we really have to go through another protracted phase of attempted customer lock-in, the way the mainframe captured customers for IBM or Windows for Microsoft. After a certain period, these lock-ins have nothing to do with return on investment and everything to do with realizing long-term profits without having to compete on a level playing field. With luck, consumers won't put up with it this time around.

Until competition arises and populates the Internet with a daisy chain of cloud data centers around the globe, we are going to live through a period of attempts at dominance cloaked as proprietary initiatives. Proprietary initiatives in a free economy are a valuable thing; they're what's bringing us the first cloud data centers. But initiative is one thing and permanent, involuntary end user ensnarement is another. At the moment, there's practically no way for cloud customers to avoid some degree of lock-in.

For example, Amazon Web Services relied on open source code that was freely available in the public arena, such as the Linux operating system and the Xen hypervisor, to build its Elastic Compute Cloud (EC2), a move that made sense because freely downloadable open source code can be replicated over and over again as the cloud scales out, without incurring license charges. Although the code was based on Xen, Amazon Web Services tweaked the file format in which its EC2 cloud's virtual machines are built. It came up with a format, the Amazon Machine Image, that was unique to EC2. The file format of a virtual machine allows it to be saved as a single file, combining the application, the operating system, and all its parts. That file, or virtual appliance, can then be stored, retrieved, and moved around like an iTune or any other digital file. Amazon has published no details on what constitutes an AMI file or how it's different from other Xen hypervisor files. But it's different enough to prevent the standard, generally available Xen hypervisor from being able to run it.

If you like sending workloads to EC2, you accept the requirement that you use AMIs and find a way to build workloads in them. But if you decide that EC2 is no longer for you, those workloads are not easily extracted and moved someplace else, unless you are able to convert them on your own into some other format, such as VMware's Virtual Machine Disk format (VMDK), Microsoft's Virtual Hard Disk (VHD), or the neutral import/export Open Virtualization Format (OVF).

In addition, Amazon's AMI format is meant for use in the EC2 cloud only. It's not available for its customers to use in their internal data centers. In the long run, Amazon will surely provide tools that will make it easy to operate a hybrid cloud between EC2 and customer data centers and migrate workloads back and forth. But as of today, that's a stumbling block.

As lock-ins go, this is a modest one and, in various multistep ways, reversible. But nevertheless, it exists as a barrier for the ill-prepared end user. To get workloads into EC2, Amazon supplies free tools to create AMIs. Tools to build AMIs are also available from independent suppliers, such as rPath. There are even vendors who will help you convert your existing virtual machines into AMI workloads, and, for a fee, RightScale, Fast-Scale, Elastra, and others will convert them or give you tools to convert them into formats that are capable of being run somewhere else. But this is not the frictionless back-and-forth migration that the cloud will need if it is to bring its full benefit to businesses. It's potential glitches and a need for services with fees attached.

There is also the previously mentioned neutral format, OVF. So far, Amazon has been noncommittal on this format. The Distributed Management Task Force standards body designed OVF to be a neutral format in which virtual machines may be moved around over the network. It is a mobility format, but the virtual machine can't actually be run in OVF. It's a freeze-dry pattern until the destination hypervisor is determined. Then OVF must be converted into that hypervisor's preferred proprietary format. A virtual machine cast in OVF can be moved under a VMware, Microsoft, or Citrix Systems hypervisor; each understands OVF and takes the files and builds them into the virtual machine of its choice. As it does so, it produces a virtual machine that is ready to run on its new host machine, unlike OVF. So the shared OVF format, which is used for importing files to a virtual machine host, represents a modest degree of cooperation among the competing vendors. As with AMIs, however, once you're in, it's hard to get out.

Why is this important? These barriers are being erected artificially. Providing a tool to convert AMIs back into OVFs would be relatively easy for Amazon, but it stays at arm's length from the prospect, just as technology pioneers before it have remained aloof from neutral formats to preserve the proprietary advantage of being ahead of the crowd. But cloud computing didn't come about as the result of a breakthrough by any single vendor. There's a large public sphere contribution to the cloud in the standards of the Internet and Web services. In the long run, lack of ease of migration is going to slow the adoption of cloud computing until end users find so many ways around it that vendors back off from their proprietary formats. No one cloud is going to be good at every form of cloud computing, so users will naturally wish to move between clouds for different jobs. In the long run, those vendors that insist that the world conform to their (and only their) standard will find it increasingly difficult to find new customers.

Many people find Amazon's EC2 a useful place to do computing and know how to build AMIs. But even these users should stay watchful. New tools or start-up vendor services will spring into being to help you convert out of AMIs into OVF or one of the other familiar virtual machine formats. A request to your Amazon representative for a reverse converter, repeated enough times, might allow the message to sink in. Customers aren't quite in the driver's seat with cloud computing, but they're much closer to it than in the previous phases of computing.

And Amazon's per hour pricing has been competitive enough to set a de facto standard that other vendors have to try to meet. Microsoft positioned its Azure hourly charges only slightly higher than Amazon's, despite the fact that Microsoft can offer a more richly tooled environment with more cloud services. By that standard, Amazon's success with AMIs has forced a major provider to a lower price point than it might have otherwise preferred.

Although the three leading x86 virtualization suppliers, VMware, Microsoft, and Citrix Systems, have agreed to support OVF, that doesn't mean that they've literally leveled the playing field among themselves. On the contrary, their support is rigged as a one-way street. Each is willing to convert a competitor's virtual machine into its own format, but it will not aid the customer in converting that virtual machine back into its original format or even back into OVF. Each supplier is thinking in terms of capturing a rival's customers, not making it easy for the customer to move workloads between clouds. In the previous phases of computing, even this modest level of cooperation would not have occurred, so OVF can be viewed as somewhat enlightened behavior. But as I say, one-way streets are just that and should not be confused with customer ease of transit.

Many people think that the possibilities of cloud computing will not be realized until there is a smooth, reliable path between the cloud and the enterprise data center and between different clouds. OVF and the current level of vendor cooperation aren't sufficient to guarantee that movement. So let the user beware. If you're a good customer of a cloud supplier, you should point out a specific purpose for which you want to use another vendor's cloud. If you get the cold shoulder, you might express some determination to find a way there—and not come back. The majority of your business is at stake. Sooner or later, the provider will get the message.

There are many reasons for businesses to adopt this demanding stance. Some cloud suppliers are specializing in setting up and tearing down software test environments, while capturing the test results (Skytap, SOASTA). Others may one day prove to be good at executing online transactions and storing those results securely. Others might provide a rich, hosted tool set for building software in the cloud (Salesforce.com, Microsoft, Engine Yard, IBM, Heroku) that will later be deployed to run in the same cloud or on Amazon's EC2. Such cloud "frameworks" can automate many underlying tasks, such as connection to the network or invoking specialized application programming interfaces, a way to speed software development.

For virtualization vendors and cloud suppliers to pretend that their customers need only one style of cloud computing (their style) is a false front. Business end users thrive on a diversity of choices, and vendors who stand in the way of diversity should be recognized as such and not rewarded. But the propensity to lock customers in remains strong.

Amazon is not alone in hanging on to the strength of a proprietary file format. The leading virtualization vendor VMware's VMDK is a proprietary format, with little information in the public sphere about it. VMware is a case where its technology strengths have kept customers from objecting too much.

Microsoft, in turn, wants to forestall VMware's dominance of the important and growing virtualization market. One of its few weapons for doing so is coordinating Hyper-V virtual machine operation in its Azure cloud with Hyper-V virtual machine operation in the enterprise data center. Doing so would allow the creation of a hybrid Windows cloud and give Microsoft's approach to virtualization an advantage over VMware's.

VMware understands the link between enterprise virtualization and cloud computing, but it is not a cloud supplier itself. It is striving to generate a similar opportunity for its customers by seeding clouds that are compatible with its virtual machine format through vCloud Express. Announced in September, vCloud Express is a set of software and tools for a cloud vendor to use in setting up low-end cloud services, including self-provisioning, billing by the hour, and load balancing hundreds of VMware-based workloads. Terremark, Bluelock, RightScale, and Hosting.com are all similar cloud service providers or front ends to other service providers, who say that they are implementing vCloud Express.

As a sign of how crucial success on this front is to VMware, it has made public its vCloud application programming interface (API), which specifies how any third party can connect to a vCloud Express supplier. It submitted a specification for vCloud Express to a standards body in the fall of 2009. That body was the Distributed Management Task Force (DMTF), the same standards group that produced OVF. VMware's submission makes its API a published specification that is headed toward becoming a public standard, a step that it hasn't taken with its virtual machine file format and other proprietary technologies. The vCloud API is the first such API from any cloud vendor to be submitted for standardization. (Fujitsu followed with its cloud API in December.)

Other cloud suppliers are seeking to capitalize on VMware's support for cloud computing. AT&T Synaptic Compute cloud,

Verizon Business, and Savvis all say that they will create more sophisticated cloud services, including in-depth security, that will host VMware virtual machines. AT&T actually launched its ability to host VMware virtual machines in June 2009. Mike Crandell, CEO of RightScale, says that his firm will create virtual machine templates that will allow a server, after it is configured by the customer, to be deployed to the cloud of the customer's choice. So far, two destinations are available: EC2 and Rackspace. In addition, RightScale will be able to configure workloads in the virtual machines of any of the three major vendors. The idea of being able to deploy servers to various clouds using different formats is likely to become a regular feature of front-end service providers.

On another front, Citrix Systems and Microsoft, who are close business partners, have both agreed to support Microsoft's VHD file format, combining the weight of the number two and number three vendors in x86 virtualization to counter VMware's better-established VMDK. Microsoft Azure will run the VHD file format. However, it's not compatible with VMware's ESX hypervisor or VMDK file format. It's the conversion problem again: VMware customers will have to find a way to convert if they are seeking a cloud based on VHD, and vice versa.

So far, few VMware customers have shown a tendency to migrate. VMware, the virtualization market leader with $2 billion in revenues in 2009, keeps advancing the capabilities of the management environment that now surrounds its virtual machines in the enterprise. Even so, the virtualization market is expanding so rapidly that it's hard to say what it will look like two or three years from now. Only 16 percent of data center applications or "workloads" have been virtualized, according to Gartner. Thus, much of the market remains up for grabs. Gartner predicts that 50 percent of data center workloads will be virtualized by 2012, so this picture is going to change.

All this competition to establish a dominant virtual file format is actually an indicator that cloud computing encourages open standards. In another bid to increase virtualization of servers with Microsoft's Hyper-V, not only has Microsoft teamed up with Citrix to back VHD, but it has also promised that VHD will remain an open format, not subject to changes that leave the customer faced with the need to upgrade to a new product and subject to new license charges. It does so with a nonbinding but highly public statement: its Open Specification Promise.

The pressure of VMware's current virtualization dominance has prompted Microsoft to adopt a stance of being more open than VMware on the virtual machine file format. The Open Specification Promise is different from actually putting a specification in the open under the authority of a standards body. Nonetheless, having some guarantee of openness, regardless of how it came about, is preferable to having a purely proprietary spec. Microsoft's stance, and its growing influence with Citrix Systems in the virtualization market, may one day force VMware to follow suit with a greater openness on its VMDK.

What's most important here is to realize that business users' virtualization choices will end up guiding their cloud decisions. When users are looking to move workloads between the data center and the cloud, compatible virtual machine formats will be an asset; incompatible ones, a drawback. The differences between VMDK, VHD, and AMI are small. They could be collapsed into one publicly referenced standard, allowing ease of migration between clouds. But that would open the dominant vendors to level playing field competition. I do not expect to see such a thing happen until cloud computing becomes widely established and the locus of competition moves to a new front. (For lock-in of a completely different sort, see Appendix C. The editor of *InformationWeek*'s "Plug into the Cloud" blog, John Foley, has illustrated how the unwary can be locked into a cloud simply by the price of trying to move one's data out.)

One way to counter the vendor's proprietary interest, however, is for customers to form groups that list their own preferences and use them to serve notice to the vendors. The best form of pressure is a paying customer pointing out the advantage of ease of movement between clouds. If this mobility is granted sooner rather than later, the immense potential of cloud computing can be realized sooner as well, and I doubt that competent vendors would be injured by such a development. User groups often produce spokespersons who are skilled at producing such a message.

In 2007, AMD's director of software development, Margaret Lewis, in a master stroke of stagecraft, if not statecraft, put representatives of VMware, XenSource, and Microsoft on stools on a raised platform at the end of a San Francisco virtualization conference, then filmed the results. Each was asked whether interoperability between their virtualization products was a good idea.

VMware's Patrick Lin, senior director of product management at the time; Microsoft's Bob Tenszar, director of product management for Windows Server; and John Bara, vice president of marketing at what was at the time XenSource (now part of Citrix Systems), all agreed that it would be better if the virtual machine formats could work together and said that they were working behind the scenes to make it happen. In a report on the occasion, I termed this evening declaration on the benefits of interoperability "virtual kumbaya." By night, we sing around the campfire; by day, we go our separate ways. Nevertheless, the big three are on the record as saying that they are working on interoperability.

Two years later, I was reminded of the backward state of the industry on this point when I attended the Cloud Computing Forum in San Francisco in February 2009 and asked a panel of cloud experts when we would achieve a shared virtual machine runtime format as well as the migration format OVF. The answers were diplomatic.

"I don't think we're holding back any genuine progress by not documenting the AMI format," said Amazon's Jeffrey Barr.

Joseph Tobolski, Accenture's director of cloud computing, who was on the panel, later backed up Barr. "Jeff's point is perfectly valid. You've got to wait until the time is right to reconcile those different formats," he said in an interview.

This panel illustrated the industry's understanding that vendors have a right to use proprietary formats until the marketplace undergoes a shakeout and everybody can tell who the winners are. If there's any reconciliation to be done, let it follow the marketplace decision.

At this event, Lewis defended virtualization vendors' practices as better than in the past. Citrix has aligned its format with Microsoft's VHD, Microsoft and Red Hat have agreed to support each other's operating systems in virtual machines, and the DMTF has published OVF, with everyone's assent. "We see our software partners working more cooperatively than they have in years. Agreements are being reached and alliances are being made," she said.

I concluded a blog entry on these responses by noting how easy it is for strong technology vendors to agree that it's reasonable to pursue their own interests, despite the fact that a simple remedy to a customer problem was at hand.

"Knowledgeable parties inside ongoing software concerns may have a disdain for those users, those small minded individuals, who just can't understand why things need to be done the way they are. But I for one say bring on those revolting end users. After this gang, I'd like to hear from them." I still think an end user revolt is one of the few ways to get powerful vendors to listen.

Rather than let this issue lie dormant, cloud users should acquaint themselves with several open source code options that are exerting pressure on the proprietary nature of cloud computing. In some cases, open source code will provide a means of knocking down closed doors and building a private cloud that interoperates with a proprietary one, regardless of whether the cloud vendor has exposed its format. Open source code may prove to be one of the ways to gain mobility between clouds.

The Eucalyptus Project, which we introduced earlier, is offering cloud APIs that can mimic what the Amazon EC2 APIs do in simple functionality, including loading a workload, calling Simple Storage Services (S3), or employing the temporary Elastic Block Store. Using these Eucalyptus APIs means that a private cloud can interoperate with Amazon's EC2. Amazon must understand that it is in its interest to tolerate this open source code as a way to extend the future reach of EC2. It has made no move to block or otherwise object to the Eucalyptus implementers.

Ubuntu, the Linux-based open source operating system from Canonical, now includes the Eucalyptus open source code as part of its package. Canonical and Eucalyptus Systems, the firm formed from the Eucalyptus Project, offer consulting services on how to build a private cloud that is compatible with Amazon's.

Eucalyptus Systems is extending what the project's original open source code can do with additional proprietary products. The Eucalyptus APIs originally supported use of open source code hypervisors only [known as Kernel-based Virtual Machine (KVM) and Xen]. The product, Eucalyptus Enterprise Edition, adds support for VMware's ESX Server hypervisor. Enterprise Edition thus could become a widely used building block of the private cloud. In the past, a wall existed between VMware's virtual machines, which are built in a VMDK file format, and EC2's Amazon Machine Image (AMI) format.

The two formats do not build virtual machines in the same way and are incompatible. The Enterprise Edition software, however, invokes a converter that changes the VMware's VMDK virtual machine into an AMI recognized by EC2. A workload in the VMware private cloud can now migrate across the boundary to function in the Amazon cloud. This opens up a path for coordination between public and private clouds.

At this point, Eucalyptus has stopped short of trying to create look-alike APIs for some of Amazon's more advanced services, such as the SimpleDB database service, Amazon Elastic MapReduce, or Amazon Relational Database Service. Nevertheless, Eucalyptus has broken down several barriers to constructing the private cloud. Because Eucalyptus is open source code, its core APIs are in the public arena.

A related effort is Simple API for Cloud Application Services, an open source project led by Zend Technologies. It seeks to provide an API for types of services that are found in the public cloud, and then let different clouds support that API, if they choose to do so. Zend's aim is to allow an application running in an enterprise to invoke, say, a Simple API for storage and receive the storage service that is available from the cloud it's dealing with—if that cloud supports Simple API. Simple API may become a way to level the playing field and give new cloud service providers a shot at attracting business from emerging private clouds. Simple API already works across the Nirvanix Storage Delivery Network, a public cloud storage provider, and Amazon's S3. That means an application built to run in one cloud could be moved to another and make use of the same services without being changed.

It's still very early in the game, but these open source initiatives show how private clouds may soon be built and find the means to synchronize their operations with public clouds. In some cases, front-end management services, such as Skytap and RightScale, already accept and manage an enterprise's virtual workloads for the cloud, even if they are generated by different hypervisors. They may extend that ability and start directly navigating the man-made barriers between private cloud operations and the public cloud.

Forces Line Up behind Cloud Standards

The Distributed Management Task Force has launched an Open Cloud Standards Incubator in which it will host early work on specifications, APIs, and other candidates to become standards of cloud computing. In November 2009, the DMTF published a 21-page white paper, "Interoperable Clouds," which makes the point that we've been emphasizing throughout this chapter: "It is important for users to use standard interfaces to provide flexibility for future extensions and to avoid becoming locked into a vendor." This white paper can be found at http://www.dmtf.org/about/cloud-incubator/DSP_ISO101_1.0.0.pdf.

The Cloud Security Alliance seeks to promote shared standards and best practices in cloud computing security. It is partnering with the DMTF to cooperate on cloud systems management standards.

Another group, the Open Grid Forum, debates proposed standards for managing large clusters known as grids and teams up with the DMTF, the Cloud Security Alliance, the Storage Networking Industry Association, and the Open Cloud Consortium to discuss standards for cloud computing. Many cloud vendors and a few cloud users belong to these groups. "Fostering trust in cloud computing services is a key criteria for enabling its growth," said Jim Reavis, cofounder of the Cloud Security Alliance. This is true, but unless these groups enlist the support of the market leaders, they will end up talking to one another as cloud customers march off to one vendor or another's proprietary drum. Too often, the open standards bodies consist of the vendors who didn't lead in a technology innovation but want a piece of the action. Open standards give them entrée to the market and allow them to invest in products that interact with those of the market leader, if they can get that leader to follow the standard.

Thus, Simple API, a potentially valuable approach to cross-cloud computing, is supported not only by little Zend Technologies, but also by IBM and Microsoft. The party that is missing among these backers is Amazon Web Services, which is by far the dominant supplier of public cloud infrastructure. The cloud customer needs to remain wary, shopping around, accepting some proprietary control when necessary to engage to the degree he wants to in cloud computing. But customers should never lose their willingness to fight lock-in.

Cloud suppliers themselves rely on the Internet, built on open standards such as Berkeley Internet Name Domain

(BIND) and Sendmail, and they frequently depend on open source code in their own infrastructure, which makes them half-open even when they'd rather not be. They understand the customer's interest in more open standards and ease of movement across vendors very well. But they won't move in that direction voluntarily. It's up to you, the cloud user, to object when they put barriers in your way. It's up to customers to pry open that door, already slightly ajar, that vendors lean against so persistently.

(((**7**)))

IT REORGANIZES

The public cloud is having a big impact on IT organizations, whether they want it to or not.

In some cases they're showing interest, although the CEO and other members of top management are still skeptical. In others, the IT organization understands the uncertainties and coming headaches that will be associated with cloud computing all too well, and it's seeking to maintain a safe distance. What are the computing professionals going to do when the CFO, who keeps hearing about the cloud's alleged efficiencies as a new paradigm, asks, "Why aren't we taking advantage of that?"

We are already in a period where those who understand the repulsion at the loose talk about the cloud's all-encompassing benefits still wish to move forward and test out its potential for their company. One person who is in an excellent position to observe the movement is Forrest Norrod, vice president and general manager of Dell's Data Center Solutions unit, which builds custom servers for large Internet companies.

Norrod says that the public cloud "has hit an inflection point where the early adopters are past the experimental phase of kicking the tires and are moving noncritical workloads into the cloud." In addition to Amazon's Elastic Compute Cloud (EC2) and Rackspace Cloud supplying servers for use by the hour in an Internet data center, several newcomers have shown up, including AT&T's Synaptic Compute as a Service, Verizon Business Cloud, and Joyent.

The interest in public clouds is spilling over into the possibility of building a similar type of operation inside the corporate data center. "We think the private cloud will start to proliferate as well. Interest is spiking through the roof," Norrod said during a visit by an *InformationWeek* team to the Dell campus in Round Rock, Texas, in early 2010 as the manuscript for this book neared completion.

Asked to describe the private cloud, he replied in jest, "It's a panacea that solves all problems." Nevertheless, he was able to describe the private cloud in a brief summary. It's a cluster of virtualized servers managed as a unit inside a company data center. The cloud cluster is able to scale up or down to meet the needs of heavily worked applications.

Norrod's business unit is a builder of customized servers, ordered in large quantities by the Internet search engine companies, such as Yahoo! and Ask.com; by Amazon Web Services; by Microsoft with its Bing search engine and Azure cloud services; and by other cloud service providers. The regular Dell organization will take what Norrod's unit has learned about cloud server design and use it to build servers for its corporate customers. When a company asks what Dell recommends for cloud servers, his Data Center Solutions group will have several proven designs as talking points.

If your company isn't one of those that are past kicking the tires, there are several ways in which an IT organization can anticipate the move to cloud computing before the business as a whole is fully committed to making the shift. There need be no subterfuge or passive resistance to other goals in such a move. On the contrary, the underlying goal of cloud computing is to provide a more flexible, manageable computing architecture with which the company can meet the challenges of the future.

To move in the right direction, regardless of whether the CEO and other members of top management have set goals and objectives, the IT staff needs to anticipate the change and build up the required skills and practices. It may do this in collaboration with business users in the ranks who need resources and may or may not realize that those resources are available through a cloudlike approach.

If the IT staff can position the company for a transition, it will come to be viewed less as an anchor that is dragging against future progress and more as a change agent that is helping the company meet the future. If the cloud pattern of computing proves to be a more flexible and economical approach, it will evolve into the general-purpose business platform. If IT is to play a consequential role in getting the company to the cloud, it is going to have to align its skills with the requirements of the new paradigm.

Even organizations that are openly contemplating using the public cloud will find that there is a need to keep many applications and much data in house. If use of the public cloud takes root, there will be a new coordination problem between its workloads and those applications that are still in-house. Indeed, one of the first new skills that IT will need to develop will be the ability to decide which application goes where.

As Norrod indicated, the early adopters are shipping "noncritical" workloads to the public cloud, those that are not essential to the day-to-day operation of the business. The software development team has a voracious appetite for resources, particularly as it nears completion of a major new application. The software must be tested in the environment in which it is to run. It must be tested with the other pieces of software on which it will depend once it's placed into day-to-day operation or "production." It must be tested against all the possible variables and combinations of events that might occur in the software stack to see if any part of it fails.

Thousands of tests chew up CPU cycles on dozens or hundreds of servers. Development teams are frequently forced to borrow some servers and acquire others in a larcenous manner (begging, borrowing, stealing) to meet their testing needs. It's the only way that they can work out the kinks and bugs in their software before it goes into production, as finding such problems belatedly carries a heavy business cost. Testing is an ideal job to ship out to the cloud, where there will be no shortage of virtual machines and the team will be charged only for the hours that they use them, not the acquisition costs.

Business applications conducting financial transactions are the opposite. They are the core of the business, the data they deal with is sensitive, and if they go down for 44 minutes, as part of an Amazon Elastic Compute Cloud (EC2) data center did recently, the loss to the business is immediate. As of today, the IT staff can't afford to let these mission-critical processes go outside its direct control and risk their going down during an outage in the cloud.

Cloud suppliers can argue that their data centers are less likely to go down than the average corporate data center. The marvelous Google search engine always seems to be available, any time of day anywhere in the world. And yet Google's widely used Gmail application experienced several short outages in 2009, prompting widespread negative reactions among its users. Google has few peers when it comes to the quality of the cloud services that it provides, so Google outages have to be taken as a warning that such events may occur with any supplier. For example, Workday, a supplier of financial management and cash management applications, experienced an outage of 15 hours on September 24, 2009. Microsoft, another supplier of online services with deep expertise and resources behind it, saw its Bing search engine go off the air for half an hour on December 3, 2009. The outage was caused by "a configuration change during internal testing," according to Microsoft. The change caused Bing to fail when it was put back in production. This type of configuration error—a human error—is one of the chief causes of outages in all data centers, and the cloud is not immune to them.

Thus, applications that deal with sensitive data, such as personal identities, financial data, and health-care data, can't be lightly sent off to run in the cloud. Doing so risks the company's compliance with Sarbanes Oxley, PCI, or HIPAA regulations. Such applications need to be posted with an off-limits sign until, at some point in the future, the security experts can guarantee secure cloud operations.

Many compute-intensive jobs fall somewhere in between these two poles. Web site logs are a treasure trove of information on how users move around the company Web site, but analyzing several months of such information is an immense computing job. The data needs to be broken down by user visit, mouse click by mouse click, until a picture of the navigation paths of many users can be seen. What path do loyal buyers take through the site, and how is it different from that taken by window shoppers and browsers? Is there a way to make the navigation path of the window shoppers lead more directly to a purchase decision? How can the decision path be made simpler and easier to navigate? At what point do browsers become buyers? Did the window shopper traffic conflict with buyers' transactions? How can the company detect such conflict and give priority to the parties that are ready to spend their money?

A minute analysis of the site, collected in many server logs, yields answers to these questions, but it requires a large amount of processing power over many hours or days. The surplus capacity frequently isn't available within the company's data center, and the task languishes.

This is a perfect example of a cloud providing a major benefit to a business. The ability to handle such analytics outside the company's data center reduces capital expense and leaves server space free for transactions and other core functions that can't be sent to the cloud.

Chances are, many organizations already have someone in-house who has some of the skills to determine which workloads should be run where. The part of the staff that has managed outside vendors or outsourcing projects will see parallel issues in managing work in the cloud. Objectives need to be well defined and service-level agreements set, with some type of independent monitoring established.

As this writer reported in *InformationWeek* on November 30, 2009, cloud computing adds its own special condition to the one-to-one nature of an outsourced project. "There's a big difference in that cloud computing runs on a shared infrastructure, so it's a less customized deal. Some compare outsourcing to renting a house and the cloud to renting a room in a hotel." The cloud user needs to take into account the risks of sharing a physical server with other users, even if each is restricted to its own virtual machines.

One way to do that is to enter into a service-level agreement (SLA) with the cloud supplier. At this stage of cloud computing, that's still an exception rather than the rule. During its first two years of beta or experimental operation, Amazon's EC2 didn't offer SLAs. It does now. Still, many users do without them, and they will find that if their application enters an infinite loop, they have little choice but to shut it down and commission another server to try again. If a server component fails and the server grinds to a halt, so does the workload. But unless you have a service-level agreement, Amazon is not responsible. The answer to the problem, its technical support tells users, is for the customer to learn how to build failover into the application, then rent a second server in EC2 to stand by as the failover destination if something happens to the first one. All of this is fair for a supplier that is providing only infrastructure, unless you've purchased an SLA that says otherwise.

Mastering this distribution of responsibility will be one challenge. Another will be meeting the CFO and CEO's expectation that the cloud is going to drive down the cost of their computing infrastructure. The CFO understands that the cloud supplier provides the capital outlay for equipment, so he's looking for reduced capital expenses while keeping operating expenses in hand.

One way to do that is to develop the capacity management skill of "cloudbursting," a name for resorting to cloud resources as a way of offloading spikes of activity that would otherwise tend to require more servers. Cloudbursting offloads a burst of activity to an infrastructure provider, where the cost of paying for a few hours of server time several times a year is far lower than that of purchasing and configuring more servers. Cloudbursting is a catchy name, but it carries its own risks. What if the cloud server fails to start as a spike of activity hits? Will that jeopardize your company's service-level agreements with your customers? What if the application starts and then goes down, losing the data that it had started to process? A small savings in capital expense can scarcely compensate for all the added time that finance will incur if it has to reconstruct the processes it was using to close the books. Any IT manager would rather spend money for another server than have a conversation with the chief of accounting, who insists on pointing out every cost incurred as a result of the downtime.

In many IT shops around the world, there's a conversation going on over the reality of cloudbursting—can the imagined savings actually materialize? No one has documented a clear answer. Yet one of the cloud's biggest allies in the face of skepticism is today's economic climate. During the downturn, it has been hard to expand or hold the line on capital budgets. It has also become unacceptable to run a server at 10 or 15 percent of capacity 95 percent of the time. Electricity is one of the highest sustained costs of running a data center, and the builders of cloud data centers have carefully positioned their facilities near cheap electricity. They've also designed many power-conserving features into their operations. One way to share in the savings is to make some use of that new cloud capacity.

Those who engage in the ambitious task of cloudbursting will want to ensure that their quickly spun up virtual machine in the cloud is actually running and doing its job. Amazon's EC2 offers a CloudWatch service, where for an additional 1.5 cents per hour per virtual server, the user can see that her virtual machine is running and delivering results. Many users will want the assurance of a monitoring service outside Amazon, such as CloudStatus.com, a monitoring service provided by VMware's Hyperic unit, the supplier of Hyperic HQ open source Web site monitoring software. CloudStatus continuously monitors Amazon's EC2 and Google's App Engine cloud.

For many IT staffs, learning how to monitor an application that is running remotely will be a new skill, and one that may require some deftness in interpreting what a cloud vendor is saying versus what your own monitoring system may be telling you. If response times sink, it will be important to know whether the problem is with the performance of the virtual server in the cloud or whether some new network latency has been introduced because a router in your path to the cloud has failed. If the cloud vendor shows a chart of perfect runtime performance, it will be important to the cloud user to have his own compilation of uptime performance statistics, in case the vendor's chart doesn't seem to apply to his particular server. If the vendor's monitoring shows 100 percent uptime, you will want your own monitoring results, showing a 30-minute outage during the previous week, to be documented and foolproof for the resulting conversation.

A new service, Apparent Networks's www.PathViewCloud .com, can provide details on the network path and network latencies involved in moving a workload to the cloud and getting results back. If the virtual machine stops running, PathViewCloud can indicate whether the problem is the network or the data center at the end of the network path your workload traveled.

Learning to monitor your virtual machines in the cloud independently will be a precursor to achieving a combined view of your virtual machines on premises and your virtual machines in the cloud. If both sets of resources could be meshed by a systems management console into one logical view, the need for staff with specialized knowledge for each environment would be reduced and some of the potential savings of cloud computing would be realized. But the cloud computing monitoring systems that are available don't have any idea what physical resources you're using on premises. That's not their job. And likewise, your on-premises systems management has only the faintest idea of what's running in the cloud.

The traditional systems management vendors, IBM, HP, CA, and BMC, are trying to mesh the views of physical and virtual resources and have at least partially succeeded. For those who don't use one of the big four, there's freely downloadable open source code from GroundWork, Zenoss, and Bluenog. However, meshing the picture you have of the on-premises data center with its related activity in the public cloud will still remain a challenge for some time.

Another fundamental change that cloud computing imposes on computer professionals is the shift in end user management. In the past, the end user has taken what the computing professionals have given him and has had little choice about it. The cloud introduces the possibility of end users provisioning themselves, and if they feel the need for an additional server, they will be able to commission another virtual machine, as long as their department pays the hourly billing expense. Users won't actually assemble and configure servers; they'll choose from a menu of possible virtual machines the one that appears best suited to their task.

It will be a key IT skill in the future to know how to map a small set of virtual machine models, make them available to end users as balanced configurations, and stick to the models for maintenance and update purposes instead of letting variations proliferate.

Such a procedure disrupts many of the IT organization's strongest beliefs about proper operation of the data center. End users historically have wanted more than the IT staff can provide, so there is a latent adversary relationship that is ready to pop up if the end users intrude too deeply into data center operations. End users getting their hands on the capability to generate virtual servers is little better than welcoming them into the data center to randomly plug in and unplug cables, network interface cards, and host bus adapters. To experienced IT professionals, the notion of end user self-provisioning is akin to the inmates taking over the asylum. That may have been the case in earlier eras of computing; in a future governed by cloud operations, however, self-provisioning is going to be a requirement. There will not be enough time or IT staff for people to drop the things they're doing because another user needs a server configured and installed.

Self-provisioning for end users can be set up through virtual machine management tools. Whether it succeeds or fails may depend on the skill with which the IT organization can design servers for different tasks. In drafting templates for virtual servers, the computer professionals will be lobbied and badgered to produce a succession of variations as end users try to satisfy every need with a unique model, and allowing them to do so will reimpose the bizarre complexity that characterized the traditional data center. Only through disciplined definition and commissioning of virtual servers can the variations in servers be limited and administrative headaches minimized, while still serving end user needs. By keeping "golden images," or well-defined, known clean copies of the virtual machine, on a secure physical server, a small IT staff will be able to spin up any number of needed virtual machines without creating a configuration challenge each time.

In fact, without user self-provisioning, the company may never reach the new era of operating with cloud-style resources. IT is going to need allies among business users who can demonstrate why the new paradigm for computing is vital to the organization. End users who experience a sudden need for server computing power can get it much more quickly by self-provisioning a virtual server than they can by setting requirements for a physical server, having IT order a model through procurement, and awaiting its building and delivery. Even after the server has been unloaded onto the loading dock, the business user is still going to have to wait for IT staffers to get to it, configure it, and load it with the right software.

Producing a virtual machine, in contrast, can be accomplished in minutes and can lead to more rapid business responses and initiatives when the situation demands it. Business users will show a marked preference for the option of self-provisioning, given the chance.

One key to making self-provisioning work will be coming up with the right set of options for end users without allowing a proliferation of designs that require frequent maintenance. Designing acceptable virtual machine servers will no longer remain the private preserve of the server's system administrator. It will take a collaboration among the system administrator, the network manager, and the security officer to produce the most viable models or templates.

In the past, each skilled staff member applied her knowledge to the task in isolation, keeping a narrow focus on one domain to preserve her depth of knowledge. Frequently, the chief security officer was the last reviewer, coming in at the last minute to insist on changes that would make a server configuration conform to security policies. A virtual machine golden image will need to get all its elements aligned right when the model is created, not in review afterward. If the number of server ports allowed is going to restrict what the server can accomplish, the network manager and the security officer are going to have to resolve what the top priority is for a particular model up front. The resulting template may serve as the basis for thousands of successive virtual machines, and any error incorporated into its final design will be replicated thousands of times.

In the view of some observers, the role of server administration will be displaced by the new importance of application administration. Server administration will move up into the layer of virtual machine monitoring and management software. Application administration will become the new focus. As noted in Chapter 3, virtualization breaks the link between an application and a particular piece of hardware, making the application mobile and capable of being migrated to different kinds of hardware.

How the application has performed at its most recent server host will be the answer sought by every IT administrator responsible for the smooth operation of the data center. Jason Hoffman, CEO of the six-year-old virtual data center provider Joyent, in San Francisco, says that the system administrator will need to become a programmer in order to survive. "The system administrator as something distinct from programmers will collapse," he predicted in an interview. A virtual data center draws on the resources of infrastructure providers and co-location service providers to give customers cloud resources through an easy-to-use front end.

An example of what he means is evident at National Retirement Partners, a San Juan Capistrano, California, firm, where the system administrator now programs in the Apex business logic language supplied by Salesforce.com. With Apex, the system administrator can now do in the Force.com cloud something that he would not have had the skills to do as a San Juan Capistrano system administrator: he can modify the standard Salesforce application so that it suits investment advisors, the professionals that he is trying to capture in the National Retirement Partners investment advisor network. That is, instead of being concerned with an on-premises server, this IT manager has produced code that helps 150 investment advisors make better use of their Force.com cloud environment.

The cloud can also reorganize IT development teams. Instead of developing software for highly specific proprietary servers in the data center, IT can now develop applications in the cloud that are destined to run in the same place where they were developed—the public cloud. The development team can be dispersed and still combine its efforts on a teamwork-produced product. The conflicts with its target environment that are so often resident in new software are resolved when the development takes place in the cloud.

In the long run, many new software capabilities will appear or, rather, reside beneath ease-of-use interfaces in the cloud. The internal IT organization will be able to develop a new application rapidly by turning to Microsoft's Azure cloud or some other cloud destination to make use of the tools there to assemble an application that is destined to run in the same cloud. Providing good software tools and making it easy to extend an existing application or pull in services from other sites and other applications will make the cloud a prime development platform, one where the business analyst or other computer-literate business user will be a coequal player with the C# or Java programmer. Business analysts can build the application they need at a given time by choosing options from a menu of application functions geared to the business analyst's domain.

In all likelihood, end users with many skill levels are going to find ways to use the resources they find in the cloud to assemble new applications and accomplish the business task in front of them. They will act on their own instead of waiting for skilled IT staffers to methodically produce new software. In the cloud, the end users will be given powerful specialized interfaces that assemble the specialized app needed in a particular business domain on command.

In the end, cloud computing will impose both a greater flexibility and new complexities on the computer professionals attempting to harness its forces. As Dell's Forrest Norrod so aptly observed, supporting the buildout of the cloud, whether public or private, "changes the economics of IT." Suddenly IT can do a lot more to enable end users to get the software they want without requiring a lot more in budget or staff resources. But it will have to reorganize with the cloud in mind and bring its best energies to bear on capitalizing on cloud resources for such a transformation to take place.

Ultimately, the cloud is a democratizing force, extending more computer resources to those whose access was formerly rationed. The degree to which IT recognizes the shift and all the potential it unleashes may determine how crucial its role will be in the next generation of computing. The bet here is that IT is one of the indispensable leaders in moving an organization from the age of constrained computer resources to the more open-ended, digital-sky-is-the-limit era of rapidly enhanced resources. To fulfill that role, the computer professional will need to be in a new and nearly coequal partnership with the end user in pushing forward all the options and initiatives of the cloud revolution.

DANGERS ABOUND: SECURITY IN THE CLOUD

We have talked thus far as if it were a simple matter to reorganize the data center into an internal cloud, offload spikes to an external cloud, and collect hundreds of thousands of dollars in savings. It may be easy to do this someday, but today this is an idealized scenario and far from the complex reality that rules a real operating data center. In fact, hazards abound.

As a multitenant facility, the cloud brings unique challenges to maintaining security, data integrity, and clean operations. Different customers, perhaps competitors, sit on the same physical server, separated by the logical boundaries of a virtual machine. New virtual machines are constantly pouring into the data center from all directions. Do any of them harbor spying agents, password stealers, or other malware? Might they end up on the physical server that you're using? Is there a risk of hardware failure if they do?

Maintaining Clean Operations and Protecting Yourself from Cloud Failure

No one knows the risk of hardware failure better than Amazon Web Services, supplier of the leading cloud service, Elastic Compute Cloud (EC2). During its first two years of beta operation, EC2 did not offer service-level agreements or guarantee continuous operation. During that period, servers froze up, virtual machines died, and workloads disappeared, but any complaints that reached Amazon Web Services were met with a stony recommendation that you architect your software to cope with hardware failures. Most IT pros are accustomed to doing the opposite: they architect the data center to avoid hardware failures.

Coping with failure in the cloud means giving your application the capability to failover to another server. The redundancy is contained and managed in the software, not the hardware. That's one of the major differences between operating in the cloud and operating in the traditional data center. One of the easiest ways to do this is to direct a failover to another nearby Amazon Machine Image (AMI), a virtual server with the same configuration as your original. In the event of a hardware failure, your data is transferred to the second server and processing picks up at the point it left off.

Amazon Web Services would probably advise you to place this failover AMI in a different zone from the original. Its data centers are divided into different "availability zones," each with independent power supplies and other resources, so that a failure in one zone doesn't take down the whole data center. Implementing this cross-zone model, however, imposes a new fee that is applied to the transfer of data between zones. You may decide that doubling what you're paying to Amazon Web Services for a second virtual machine is enough. You don't want to incur more secondary costs. You leave your backup machine in the same zone as the original, as there's no fee to transfer data within the zone.

If you've made such a decision, consider this incident on December 9, 2009. A component of the power supply for a zone of Amazon's data center in the US-East-1 region, in this case, northern Virginia, failed, and Amazon eventually alerted customers to this event. Several zones make up a region, so it would be hard to tell from this information where the data center was or whether your virtual machine was running in it. If you did not employ either Amazon's CloudWatch service, which monitors your virtual machine and indicates when it stops running, or a third-party service, such as VMware Hyperic's CloudStatus service, you probably wouldn't know that your virtual machine had stopped running until it failed to deliver the expected results.

If you heard through the grapevine that an Amazon EC2 zone was down, you could go to the online Amazon Service

Health Dashboard. Amazon regularly reports on the status of its services through the dashboard. It uses a little green icon to indicate that a service is functioning normally or a yellow one to indicate a problem. Normally, the dashboard is littered with rows of continuous green symbols.

On December 9, at 4:08 a.m. Eastern time, Amazon posted a warning symbol with information that indicated, "We are investigating connectivity issues for instances in the US-East-1 region." Such information is frustratingly nonspecific to the cloud user. But there was more. Eighteen minutes later came the notice, "We are experiencing power issues . . . in a single availability zone in the US-East-1 region." What had happened, according to subsequent notices, was that a primary power supply component had failed. "Prior to completing the repair of this unit, a second component, used to assure redundant power paths, failed as well, resulting in a portion of the servers in that availability zone losing power," Amazon Web Services posted to its dashboard.

These notices give the EC2 cloud a degree of transparency, a prized attribute in cloud operations, but if an individual customer depended on them alone, his view into his virtual machines would be far from transparent—somewhere between translucent and opaque.

In fact, the user needs to maintain some independent view into cloud operations to know whether her virtual machines are running or stalled. As it turns out, a new service, Apparent Networks' PathViewCloud, had been in operation for about a month, and it tracked the service outage to a router on the

Internet in the northern Virginia area. The outage started at 12:34 a.m. Pacific time, according to Apparent, 34 minutes before the dashboard reported a problem. It ended 44 minutes later, at 1:19 a.m. Pacific. The posts to the Service Health Dashboard indicated an ongoing problem until 1:51 a.m., when the post, "The underlying power issue has been addressed. Instances have begun to recover," appeared. The initial notice was late, but to be fair, the notice of recovery trailed the start of the actual recovery by 32 minutes as well, according to Apparent's information.

The information that Amazon makes available when such incidents occur seems to be aimed at minimizing the problem rather than acknowledging its scope. It may be put there by someone who is busy solving the problem, not by someone who is on standby with nothing to do but explain mishaps to the public. In short, Amazon Web Services achieves a high degree of translucency with its Service Health Dashboard, but full transparency is too much to expect from your cloud provider. This is very different from data center operations, where the people who answer questions can be fired by the people who are asking them. In the data center, obviously, the facilities are directly under a company's control.

On the other hand, Amazon Web Services representatives may debate my statement that postings tend to minimize the severity of the problem. The second notice, at 1:26 a.m. Pacific time, stated that the data center managers were experiencing "power issues for a subset of instances in a single availability zone." This sounds like a contained outage, possibly a minor incident. Apparent Networks, a network performance monitoring company, however, monitors network performance by using more than one account per cloud data center. In the northern Virginia outage, Apparent Networks had 20 accounts running virtual machines with EC2, and 6 of the machines, or 30 percent, were unavailable. Its executives are careful to say that they can't tell whether a similar percentage of all customer accounts were affected by the outage.

"On the whole, Amazon is extremely consistent" in both steady data center operations and reporting incidents as they occur, said Javier Soltero, CTO of management products at VMware. He is the former CEO of Hyperic, the company behind the open source code system that monitors cloud services and is the basis for the free service at www.CloudStatus.com. In the Amazon outage, he concedes, "We see a gap," or a delay between the occurrence of the incident and the time it was reported. Whether that was due to the staff workload required to fix the problem, a preference for getting a handle on an incident before saying anything, or some other reason, "only people at Amazon know for sure," he said.

But the failure of both primary and backup power supplies in EC2 should teach the unwary customer a lesson: keep your recovery system in the cloud in a separate zone from your primary system.

Like other EC2 terms, a zone means something specific to Amazon Web Services, but there's not necessarily a clear definition of the zone involved in this incident. The explanation I received in a December 12 e-mail from Amazon said: "Availability Zones are distinct locations that are engineered to be insulated from failures in other Availability Zones and provide inexpensive, low latency network connectivity to other Availability Zones in the same Region. By launching instances in separate Availability Zones, a user can protect their applications from failure of a single location. Regions consist of one or more Availability Zones." This points out another need in cloud computing—a shared language so that each side knows what the terms being used mean.

I've spent some time on Amazon's outage because it illustrates several things about how cloud operations work and don't work. All the concerns that come to light with regard to basic operations, then, are going to be magnified several times when it comes to privacy and security. The Cloud Security Alliance urges in unvarnished terms that users should not assume that cloud computing operates with all the layers of protection that a business normally enjoys. Servers that you're using in the cloud are somewhat analogous to servers running on your Web site. They're just outside the protected perimeter of the business, with a Web server port or ports open to all browser calls, all traffic, all comers.

Assume That the Cloud Is Less Secure Than Your Data Center

IT managers call this area the DMZ, or demilitarized zone, between, figuratively speaking, two competing parties on the Web, in this case, a business on one side and the public on the other. The "public" includes a certain number of virus writers, script kiddies, and malware planters.

The Web server can handle traffic coming to it, but it holds that traffic there, denying it entry to corporate systems. Only through its own protected procedures does it access internal resources. The data center is separated from the DMZ behind a deeper set of protective layers, primarily firewalls that screen traffic, filters that keep out specific unwanted message sets, and intruder detection systems that look for invasive agents. The screens protect the database servers, business production systems, and other systems that make the business run.

Amazon's EC2 is the form of cloud computing known as infrastructure as a service (IAAS), where users load remote server hardware in a data center on the Internet with the workload that they want to run. They exercise programmatic control over the operation of the virtual machine, known as an Amazon Machine Image. In some ways, it looks and feels like a duplicate of what you're doing in the data center. You trust the cloud provider, whether it's Amazon Web Services, Rackspace, or Verizon Business, to supply security at the perimeter of its operations.

Cloud providers encourage this thinking. In a recent incident, someone who was probably a professional thief succeeded in placing a botnet, or a remotely controlled agent, on a legitimate host and used it to serve as a control center for pursuing users' bank account information. The Zeus botnet, as it was called, had been placed on a Web site being hosted in Amazon's EC2, the first such known invasion of EC2 by a botnet.

After I reported on this incident for *InformationWeek* on December 11, 2009, Amazon spokesmen Kay Kinton responded: "Users of Amazon EC2 use the same precautions to secure and protect their Web site as they do with traditional hosting solutions, so it is no easier for potential abusers to compromise Amazon EC2 based Web sites. . . . We were able to locate the Zeus botnet controller and promptly shut it down. We take all claims of misuse of the services very seriously and investigate each one. When we find misuse, we take action quickly and shut it down."

All of this is to Amazon Web Services' credit, but it also makes clear that it's impossible to keep all malware out of the cloud. Variants of the Zeus botnet are believed to have been responsible for the theft of $100 million from bank accounts in 2009. The Cloud Security Alliance, in a white paper released last April, says, "Hosts running within an infrastructure-as-a-service are akin to hosts running in the DMZ of your enterprise's network." Cloud service providers would say that that's too harsh, but for now, it's a good warning.

The most disquieting concerns about computing on infrastructure as a service are the things that we lack years of solid experience in dealing with—multiple virtual machine servers running on one physical piece of hardware is a relatively recent phenomenon in the data center. As noted in Chapter 3, the ability to manage servers flexibly in this manner leads to many of the basic ideas of cloud computing. But there remain troubling questions.

When an intruder gets onto a server, intrusion detection systems know where to watch for activity and have well-defined patterns of software event sequences that tell them that something is amiss. But the operation of the virtual machine, an application with its own operating system, is a different realm of vulnerability. There are frequently many moving parts in a virtual machine, including code libraries and middleware as well as the application and its operating system. Thousands of end users are building their own Amazon Machine Images (AMIs), with operating systems that may or may not have the latest protective measures. Depending on the skill with which they've been written, applications offer their own avenues of attack through buffer overflows, SQL injection, and other forms of attack where malicious code is entered in place of the names, dates, and other familiar information. Applications can be composed to protect against such intrusions, but have they been in every instance in the cloud? Who polices all this activity?

Amazon provides instructions on how to build an AMI and urges prospective customers to also use their own precautions. "Your listing will show up on the site after a quick review by AWS," says the Web page Amazon Web Services, Submit an AMI (http://developer.amazonwebservices.com/connect/kbcategory/.jspa?categoryID=116). How much critical scrutiny is included in that "quick review"?

In the cloud, these virtual machines are going to reside on the same physical server as yours. This is widely viewed as a safe practice within a self-contained corporate data center, but will the same be said of operations outside its walls a few years from now? The online *MIT Technology Review*, in its October 23, 2009 report "Vulnerability Seen in Amazon's Cloud Computing," said that a study had concluded that it was technically feasible for a skilled agent to put a virtual machine into EC2 on the same server as one occupied by someone on whom it wishes to snoop. Virtual machines have IP addresses that are "visible to anyone in the cloud." Address numbers that are close together are often sharing the same hardware in EC2, the *Review* said, so through trial and error, a snooper could try to place one of its virtual machines on the same servers.

"It is possible to carefully monitor how access to resources fluctuates and thereby potentially glean sensitive information about the victim," said the report. It didn't make it clear what information might be gleaned from resource use, but many security researchers have worried that it would be possible for one virtual machine to spy on another if it could watch the activity of the hypervisor. All virtual machines on the same physical server share one hypervisor, and each virtual machine's calls for hardware services must pass through the hypervisor.

In the same report, Eran Tromer, a postdoctoral researcher in MIT's Computer Science and Artificial Intelligence Laboratory, and three colleagues from the University of California at San Diego said that such a snooping attack was more likely to succeed if the listener generated his virtual machines at the same time as the target did. If a potential target company is running its Web site in the cloud, the snooper could flood the site with activity, prompting it to start up more virtual machines. The attacker would then create virtual machines at the same time and have a good prospect of landing on the same physical server, Tromer said.

One possible use for such a position would be to "listen to" an idle virtual machine nearby in order to sense activity on the server when it starts up. A small spike in activity might indicate that a user was typing a password into the virtual machine's application. If keystrokes within the spike could be detected by the level of activity on the server, then in some cases the timing of the keystrokes would reveal the password, he said. That is, certain letters are habitually struck closer together or farther apart than others, a perhaps tenuous detection method. But the security researchers say that it can be made to work.

Other "side-channel information" inferred from listening techniques could reveal a great deal about a target. Tromer's team probed EC2 to reach its conclusions, and he was quoted by the *Review* as saying, "We firmly believe these vulnerabilities are generic to current virtualization technology and will affect other [cloud] providers as well." The technique where someone seeks to map a cloud to find a target of choice is called "cartography."

Amazon's spokeswoman Kay Kinton responded to these claims. "The side channel techniques presented are based on testing results from a carefully controlled lab environment with configurations that do not match the actual Amazon EC2 environment. As the researchers point out, there are a number of factors that would make such an attack significantly more difficult in practice." She also said that Amazon has put safeguards in place that prevent attackers from using such cartography techniques.

Other writers, such as Nitesh Dhanjani, writing on the O'Reilly open source blog, OnLamp.com, say that there's an implicit threat in any given cloud where thousands of virtual machines are being reproduced based on one model. He calls it the "threat of mono-culture." In a virtual machine monoculture, such as look-alike AMIs, a vulnerability contained in one "will apply to all other instances of the same image. If an exploitable vulnerability is found in the kick start image of AMIs, then the security of a considerable amount of resources and data will be at stake."A solution, he suggests, is for customers to build their own AMIs and then move them into the cloud under conditions where Amazon Web Services doesn't have the right to review them. This approach is sometimes referred to as a zero-knowledge-based solution and insists on keeping the cloud owner's hands off the user's clean version of an AMI.

The cloud's nightmare scenario, however, is that a skilled hacker finds a way to access the "ec2-terminate-instance" service, a command to halt a running virtual machine, "and finds a way to apply it to all instances in its zone." Widespread virtual machine interruptions and damage might result. "Such a vulnerability could be abused to black out the Amazon cloud," Dhanjani wrote on April 27, 2008.

The Cloud Security Alliance, in an April 2009 white paper, agreed: "IaaS providers make a vast number of virtual machine images available to their customers. [A virtual image] should undergo the same level of security verification and hardening as it would for hosts within the enterprise," it warned. In other words, if you take what a cloud vendor gives you, upgrade it to the same degree of hardness and protections that you would implement in-house before using it.

Then it suggests something that I believe will become a best practice in the design of virtual machines (sometimes referred to as virtual appliances) to run in the cloud. Both the application and its operating system should be stripped down to the essentials needed to do the job intended for a specific workload. "Limiting the capabilities of the underlying application stack not only limits the overall attack surface of the host, but also greatly reduces the number of patches needed to keep that application stack secure," the alliance's white paper stated.

In addition, a word needs to be said for Amazon's own practices. When it accepts a virtual machine to run on its servers, it equips that machine with its own firewall, a best practice for running virtual machines in any environment. The firewall can detect malware and shield the virtual machine from it. Amazon also issues a digital key to the virtual machine's application to identify it as a valid account. The key is passed as the application calls for cloud services or communicates across nodes in the cloud to other parts of the application. This practice makes it much harder for an intruder to mimic the application and get at its data or gain responses reserved for the application.

Some firms are beginning to specialize in virtual machine security; they promise to upgrade the levels of protection on virtual machines moving around the Internet. One of them is Altor Networks. Todd Ignasiak, director of product management, points out that cloud computing presents "a particularly juicy target" for professional hackers who are interested in stealing passwords, bank account information, and personal identities because of all the activity that is going on in a concentrated setting. Furthermore, the malware author can sometimes arrive hidden in the traffic of a legitimate activity, as happened with the Web site hosting the Zeus botnet referred to earlier. Hackers prefer to be cloaked behind legitimate operations where they are harder to detect and leave fewer tracks.

But the biggest security danger in the cloud is one that hasn't been recognized yet, at least not publicly, to anyone's knowledge. The virtualization hypervisor is a central piece of software through which virtual machines on a physical server must obtain their hardware services. All communications between virtual machine operating systems and the hardware pass through the hypervisor, and from that vantage point, a skilled agent could discern the activity of each and every virtual machine. A relatively new product, the hypervisor firewall with intruder detection, is available through Altor and several other suppliers to guard this sensitive position.

As in intruder detection elsewhere, the watchdog on the hypervisor is looking for departures from known patterns of events that represent a norm, sequences of events that signal that an intruder is at work, or a strange new pattern from the hypervisor that indicates that it has started to do something that is outside its assigned role.

The hypervisor also manages the virtualized server's virtual switch, which does in software what a physical switch does on the physical network: it routes I/O traffic and storage traffic to individual virtual machines and handles communications between them. If an intruder could somehow get control of the virtual switch, she would be in a position to spread agents or malware to other virtual machines, not only on the host physical server, but also on other virtualized servers that the host's virtual machines have permission to talk to.

Ignasiak, of course, favors widespread adoption of Altor's virtual firewall for the hypervisor. Regardless of whose product is used, it's essential that the operations of this central piece of software be protected through ongoing research and constant upgrade of what its firewall/intruder protection system can do.

In addition to IaaS, cloud computing is sometimes delivered in the pattern known as platform as a service, or PaaS. The platform is the computer server and services infrastructure, similar to Amazon's, but the customer is also offered additional tools and building blocks to extend an application on the cloud platform or build a new one to run on the platform. While an AMI exists on its own, a platform application might get the services of an enterprise service bus that can automatically link it to other applications. It would also gain services from integration software that can convert data from one source into the format required by another.

The Cloud Security Alliance warns, however, that platform extensions and building blocks for applications mean that the applications must take a greater share of responsibility for security in the cloud environment than they would in an enterprise environment. Existing Web applications "have a rich body of knowledge about common types of vulnerabilities and their mitigation. Similar knowledge for platform-as-a-service environments must still be developed," it warns.

The third common form of cloud computing is software as a service, or SaaS, with Salesforce.com and its popular customer relationship management (CRM) application being a leader in this space. Without Salesforce.com's ability to establish the concept of the multitenant application—that is, software running as a service with thousands of simultaneous users—there would be far less interest in cloud computing today than it currently enjoys.

Software as a service has many integration points with applications back in the corporate infrastructure and offers the option of customers building custom objects that work with the supplier's application set. A customer of SaaS must be aware of what security precautions his vendor has built into the SaaS services. He needs to establish for himself that the data generated in SaaS applications is securely stored in the SaaS environment and remains transferable to him on demand. In extending SaaS applications with custom objects, the customer must adhere to the programming and security conventions demanded by the vendor's computing platform or risk disrupting the vendor's cloud.

When Salesforce.com scrutinizes a customer submission, it is with an eye to strict adherence to its stated allowances. The customer must be "especially concerned about the software development lifecycle" of its SaaS supplier, says the Cloud Security Alliance. That is, is the supplier acting in a timely manner to deal with new threats and staying abreast of the state of the art in protecting the service from hackers?

As we have seen, each form of cloud computing carries its own risks, options, and rewards. In this young industry, it's still caveat emptor, but at the same time early adopters will be rewarded with experience in how cloud computing works and where competitive advantage might flow from its cost structure. The current shallow trust boundaries within the cloud are going to be pushed back to allow more and more trusted interactions.

When it comes to the cloud, the run book—the document of best practices—is still being written. In its place, the school of direct experience may be the only way to find out some of the things you need to know. The risks are clearly there, but in most instances the risks can be defined, evaluated, and contained for certain workloads. There are still questions about some elements of secure virtual machine operation, but impressive resources are being poured into researching the danger points. Improved solutions are sure to be put in place, and one by one, the barriers to sound operations will fall.

(((**9**)))

YOUR CLOUD STRATEGY: WHAT KIND OF COMPANY DO YOU WANT?

The growth of cloud computing outside companies will change computing practices inside companies. But having adapted to some of the efficiencies and conventions of the cloud, can an IT organization change the rest of the company?

In all likelihood, by itself, it cannot. A business's habits, processes, and conventions of thinking are embedded in what has worked for it in the past. The computing professionals can only make cloud computing available as a potential platform for the business. Here's where every business professional has something to contribute in making the transition. New uses of computing will spring up continually as cloud resources grow.

Computer-literate business users will increasingly gain mastery of these uses, in some cases taking advantage of new ease-of-use features available through the cloud. If the use of these features is misunderstood or minimized by the organization as a whole, users should point out how other companies are gaining competitive advantage from their own use of the cloud.

One of the most basic business values that the cloud will tend to overturn is the perception that major computer resources are expensive and are reserved for a specially trained cadre of database administrators and business intelligence experts that know how to use them. The name "glass house," denoting the data center, came into being because of the special air-conditioning requirements that computers have tended to demand, along with a desire to keep the average employee away from the cables, cords, and buttons that control them. It has simply followed that major data center resources are to be husbanded stringently. Whatever the virtues of that attitude at one time, it's now a liability. The walls of the glass house need to dissolve into the constantly accessible, user self-provisioning internal cloud.

Whatever a given amount of x86 server power cost last year, it will cost half as much next year as the 24-month cycles of Moore's law continue their inexorable march. No matter how you do the math, throwing more computer power this year than last year at a well-conceived design, a well-planned customer analysis, or a well-targeted campaign is going to be a good investment. This is not the same as building an expensive, high-performance computing center. With public clouds, you can apply a large cluster of servers to a problem for a few hours or a few days a month at a price that most companies can afford. This is an unheralded, revolutionary change in the business landscape, one that applies to global competition, and its ramifications have yet to be fully understood.

If you don't get into the habit of making use of large amounts of resources, if you stick to the attitude that computing power is a scarce and precious resource, your company will be outflanked by those that figure out how to tap into the cloud. Some companies will encourage their employees to use lots of computer power on promising ideas. Others will hold back, pointing to the critics who say that the cloud may not be a paradigm shift, or that it may turn out to be more expensive than the "enthusiasts" think. For that matter, I know of no academic study that establishes the cloud's economies of scale beyond a shadow of a doubt. So let's keep an open mind on the evidence. The people who bet that cloud computing will be as expensive as or more expensive than corporate data centers have missed out on the way cloud data centers leave their predecessors' expensive complexities behind. Critics fail to understand the rapid productivity gains that flow from virtualizing a cluster of servers and managing them as one large computer—remember the Google engineer's concept, "The Data Center as a Computer."

Users May Seek Generous Cloud Use; What's Wrong with That?

It is intuitive to many, although not yet proven, that the cloud has the potential to do for business computing what the Internet did for private corporate networks—provide a publicly available resource that is big enough for nearly any task, at commodity prices. Skepticism about the cloud exists, but leading implementers will prove its feasibility.

Every major technology firm believes in the future of cloud computing—Microsoft, IBM, Google, Amazon.com, HP, Sun Microsystems, Dell, Gartner, Accenture, and others. Start-ups in Silicon Valley, notoriously long on computer skills and short on cash, all believe in it. And early adopters have been opting for more of it. In 2009, Amazon.com's use of network bandwidth in renting cloud computing infrastructure on the Elastic Compute Cloud surpassed its bandwidth use in online retailing. It's a remarkable new business for a company that was already one of the most successful Internet businesses.

Every organization that adopts the practice of generously tapping computing resources, whether they're in the internal cloud or the public cloud, will incur some waste, compared to the previous generation. Someone will try a poorly aimed marketing campaign or test a design that never had a chance of getting off the ground. But to some extent, that's a prerequisite for the organization's new approach to computing. Software exists to mimic the events of the real world in binary logic, and today's software does a better job of it than ever before. With access to cloud resources, more models and simulations can be conducted as a prelude to launching new products or services in the real world. The possibilities of the virtual world are growing in importance as cloud resources become available.

Management still needs to police excesses, but executives who demote or fire someone for using an hour too much cloud server time will have a bad effect on the general sense of experimentation. The resource has to be treated as generously available to those who have shown that they have a knack for using it, or who merely show the prospect of having the knack. It can't be reserved for a high priesthood, as in the past. Experimenting with cloud resources is going to be necessary for the day when cloud computing is commonplace and your company will need to maintain an environment of constant modeling, experimentation, and trial-and-error test implementations to survive. It will need a staff of computer-literate, or perhaps just cloud-literate, experimenters to do so.

In the outside world, the cloud revolution will already be mobilizing millions of end users to do more with the newly available computer power. The power in their handheld, laptop, or desktop machine will be amplified by specific services in the cloud that they can access and resources that they can drive. The primary interaction between a business and its customers will occur in the cloud, and that interaction will be far richer than today's shallow exchange over the Web. Yes, Amazon.com can tell you what other books were bought by other purchasers of the volume that you just acquired. But in the cloud, a rich profile of who those customers are will be available, along with business intelligence on what they have been buying recently, how well the products have worked for them, what their service calls and complaints have been, and what might be needed by their businesses in the future. If a customer has had a recent unresolved complaint, that will be the first—not the last—thing acknowledged in any exchange, human or machine-based. The customer might pour more information on the complaint into the exchange, or the customer service rep might cite the results from customers who have had a similar problem and apply automated diagnostics to the product, with more back and forth over the specifics of the customer's environment. Maybe the problem is resolved; maybe the customer merely gets a sense that someone is paying attention and it will be resolved soon.

The Cloud Economy

The future economy will knit together information services and goods by integrating previously separate functions. In such an economy, being stingy with computer cycles will equate less to the wise use of resources and more to missed opportunities. Every now and then, some unexpected bonus springing from the consistent use of the cloud will offset by many times the occasional excess use of it.

In short, the cloud revolution doesn't lead to excess and waste in Internet server usage, as critics might suppose. On the contrary, it leads straight to the cloud economy, where information rolls up a value chain until it can be combined into new goods and services that seemed impossible a short while ago. Instead of the cloud economy, this might be characterized as the post-dot-com phase of the Internet economy, where the formerly mesmerizing goal of traffic for traffic's sake has been replaced by real, integrated business function.

Whatever you call it, the economy is clearly moving toward information-based services, delivered inexpensively and rolled up into sophisticated combinations that make it easier for individual businesses to cope with a complex world.

Take, for example, Adam Sokolic, senior vice president of operations at National Retirement Partners: Financial Advisors. His San Juan Capistrano, California, firm provides its own unique analysis of mutual funds to advisors of pension and retirement fund managers; it's an investment advisor to investment advisors, and as such it occupies a rarefied niche where the stakes are high and competition is keen. National Retirement has formed its own network of independent advisors, who use additional National Retirement tools and services. Its 150 members are a growing force among retirement fund and pension fund managers. Each time Sokolic can recruit another advisor into the fold, it increases the use of his firm's analysis tools and his return on analysis services investment.

In an interview, Sokolic said that a key part of his business strategy is to be both a consumer and a provider of cloud services. He bases much of his business on the customer relationship management (CRM) and other software as a service applications provided by Salesforce.com. These applications run on large server clusters in Salesforce.com's data center, and are accessed over the Internet by their users. Members of the National Retirement Partners network are supplied with tools that customize the standard customer relationship management app. With National Retirement's additions, advisors can find prospects for the particular type of investment knowledge or compliance knowledge that they represent.

When National Retirement recruits independent advisors to its network, it shows them a custom Salesforce.com CRM application that they can use (after they sign up for a Salesforce .com account). Sokolic shows the added value of the network by asking for a type of pension or retirement fund manager that the advisor would like to contact. He then directs his customer CRM app "to pull 1,200 names into a lead prospect list" that meets those criteria. "It's a major 'Wow!' for them. Such a list doesn't exist anywhere else," he said.

Sokolic said that his firm will keep producing custom tools for his network members' CRM app. The resulting application runs in the cloud like one of Salesforce.com's own, but it gives the advisor leverage that other advisors without the same tools don't have. Sokolic's success at using the cloud to extend what his six-year-old firm can do has resulted in National Retirement coming in at number two on *Inc.* magazine's list of 500 fastest-growing companies in 2009. It was number 97 in 2008.

National Retirement uses a customized CRM application as a major recruiting tool to bring advisors into its network. The members of the network, in turn, share some data and best practices with National Retirement, enhancing the San Juan Capistrano firm's big-picture knowledge of the market.

Sokolic doesn't have a big IT budget or staff with which to do this. On the contrary, he has a staff of three. Without the assistance of the cloud platform, he could not be nearly as competitive as he is in the investment advisor market. With the Salesforce.com cloud services, National Retirement is able to achieve a crucial degree of integration with its 150 independent network members that it could never have achieved if it needed to integrate systems in 150 different offices. By leaving behind the problems of individual data center complexity and relying on the standards imposed by the cloud, National Retirement can supply crucial information to its advisors, while aggregating valuable market data from them, for a fraction of the noncloud cost. In National Retirement's business, an analysis service is the backbone of the business, but auxiliary services, added at low cost to software as a service CRM, are what make it grow faster than its competitors. Each time it expands these services, National Retirement makes it easier for the advisors in its network to offer clients more information and run their offices in a more automated way.

This is an early example of the cloud economy. Information that is of low value to one advisor gains value as it is aggregated with information from other advisors. New software from National Retirement is added to a standard CRM package that is available in the cloud, which can pull nuggets from the aggregate for the individual advisor. Accomplishing this with a limited budget and a small IT staff has set National Retirement apart. Soon the cloud economy will be setting other firms apart as they get astride its capabilities.

Another way of saying this is that the cloud is an ideal software development and integration platform. Tools provided in the cloud can simplify the development of software to be run in the cloud and accessed there by many users. Salesforce .com is rapidly adding such tools. Simplicity disrupts complexity and beats it in a competitive race.

What You Can Do to Get Started: Social Networking

A more basic example of what will happen on a regular basis will be workplace social networking, which can shorten lines of communication and bring together necessary talents in an organization that often has departmental boundaries keeping them apart. Social networking is already a fixture at most businesses in one rudimentary form or another, usually set up by IT at the direction of the top. It might consist of a company wiki, where various topics are aired and commented upon. Social networking is already a consumer phenomenon in the form of MySpace, Facebook, and LinkedIn. It doesn't require "the cloud" to be implemented, but it's more likely to yield a payoff if it's available as an employee self-provisioned service. It's one thing to have a service set up by a distant boss, and another when you and a freshly minted but geographically dispersed team really need one.

It will not be hard for employees to commission a social networking site if IT has succeeded in starting a rudimentary cloud in the data center. Employees in different departments and locations, responding to some pressing need, could establish a wiki, where individuals share what they know on a current business challenge, comment frequently on developments, establish a document library, and assemble a database of known information. One of the main benefits of such a wiki site is that it allows others in the organization who have knowledge of or interest in the same topic to search it out and share what they know. That sounds simple, but in fact all kinds of hierarchical, departmental, geographical, and role-assigned boundaries tend to inhibit it from happening in many business settings. "Social networking cuts across these artificial boundaries to 'flatten' communications," concluded Arthur Jue, Jackie Marr, and Mary Ellen Kassotakis in *Social Media at Work.*

In addition to people finding out what others know, an aggregation system could combine e-mail threads and tie together individual conversations to be sent to a group list.

The wiki site could regularly conduct searches for any relevant documents, sales materials, Web site references, conference presentations, and other such material that may spring up inside the company. In short, the wiki becomes an aggregator of what the company knows on the topic, with a few active voices taking the lead on what to do with the information. Some outspoken members of the group might start blogs and publish what they know on a daily basis. In this manner, a collaborative knowledge comes into being that no one in the company realized was already there. Gaps are identified. Leading voices are identified. A network forms and creates an ad hoc team to cope with an important change.

An adjoining function for a social networking server would be recruitment. A Web page dedicated to "the team" could post the background and previous projects of those participating, including projects at other companies that fellow workers previously knew nothing about. References to people both inside and outside the company become part of the discussion. The site becomes a recruitment station, where those who are interested start contributing their experience and what they think needs to happen next.

And it's likely to display what Jue et al. termed "unexpected reach," or the ability to find people with information related to the project that management or other members of the team knew nothing about. Fresh talent can find the team by searching on a subject from a source in the internal cloud and finding references to the group's activity. It allows those who can contribute to volunteer from the shadows. In the face-to-face world, well-established hierarchies tend to inhibit such behavior. There will be chaff produced in this process, perhaps, from wannabes and posers, but the group is likely to function with a collective intelligence on what is real and what is tertiary.

An example of where this type of digital crossroads and intense social networking works in real life is open source code projects. A project site is set up, and developers from around the world comment freely on the nature of the task and the quality of the code. The project has a continuous string of comments from participants and responses from those responsible for specific areas of the project and the project leaders, who hold their positions largely as a result of their skill in both producing code and coordinating the efforts of others. The active process of producing and reviewing code becomes a filter through which many participants come to be viewed, even though the project leader knows little else about them.

A rough democracy prevails; the code is the thing, and ability to contribute to the code is one of the few criteria that are used to determine status in the group. The level playing field that is created and the transparent communications used bring out extraordinary effort by skilled programmers, who suddenly find themselves in their element, unfettered by the usual requirements of meetings, planning, and coordination. And they enjoy it. The project to develop the Linux operating system, the Apache Web server now predominant on the Web, and Samba translation software between Linux and Windows are all ongoing examples.

The cloud is not required for social networking or collaborative development, but in a business setting, where things need to happen fast, the cloud style of computing will be a huge enabler of collaborations of many types, including collaborative design and development.

In a more general sense, social networking sites at work can help segment out attributes in an otherwise undifferentiated workforce. In *Social Media at Work*, Arthur Jue, Jackie Marr, and Mary Ellen Kassotakis argue that the underlying purpose of creating social networking sites is "connecting people who were previously unaware of each other." That seems obvious enough, and yet it is a fundamental change in the business world, where people usually have to be of equal status in the business to talk frankly about problems or challenges.

If a social networking site brings together people who are interested in the same thing, those people will also exhibit, in a business context, a key attribute of the consumer site, which is that social networking sites "are sticky as users keep coming back to them to check up on friends and acquaintances." Everyone saying what she thinks on a wiki or community forum site may seem chaotic to a traditional manager, but the group as a whole is sorting the information and seeing who stands out, who guides the discussion at critical moments, and who has a sustained drive to address the topic. This is one of many tasks of the traditional middle manager, but as many of us know, their knowledge was limited, sometimes prejudiced, and difficult to convert into action. Furthermore, there are a lot fewer of them around, good or bad. In the slimmed-down lean corporation, social networking is going to have to serve as one of the substitutes. It will allow employees to get new ideas, learn something that will solve a problem, and in general share in the knowledge of how the business is supposed to work.

If you do not believe this, consider the fact, now long established in Silicon Valley, that many of the most successful companies have two equal cofounders. Bill Hewlett and David Packard formed HP in a garage in Palo Alto. Steven Wozniak and Steve Jobs, two men with vastly different skills and personalities, formed Apple Computer in another garage. Sergey Brin and Larry Page formed Google and collected $100,000 in investment before they had a bank account in which to deposit it. The modern Amazon.com with Amazon Web Services is the creation of both Jeff Bezos and CTO Werner Vogels, who has pushed hard toward the Web Services and EC2 cloud business.

Ann Winblad, a venture capitalist with Hummer Winblad Venture Partners in San Francisco, looks for such teams that are still at an early stage of company formation and considers them strong prospects for success. One of the reasons is that they stay on course more easily than a solitary founder by himself. The two partners trust each other, have short immediate lines of communication, "and one seems to have a veto power over the bad ideas of the other," she noted at a venture capital gathering three years ago. That veto power, I believe, is an example of the power of social networking in concentrated form. The group, when plugged into a competitive threat or intriguing opportunity, has a self-correcting compass when attempts are made to drive it off course.

A company can use social media to pull talent out of the shadows and put it to work at a higher level; recruit talent from inside or outside the organization to help with that effort; allow competent employees with similar levels of involvement in the business to find each other, share both gripes and a sense of opportunities, collaborate, and redesign what's already been designed; and give people on the margins a greater engagement through a stake in the direct future of the company.

Paul Gillin, author of *The New Influencers: A Marketer's Guide to the New Social Media* (Quill Driver Books of Linden Publishing, 2007) reached a similar conclusion. He cited the apparent chaotic nature of blogs, which were proliferating in the 2005–2007 period, with some writers predicting the spread of virulent backbiting and misinformed commentary. Instead, Gillin pointed out that the blog writers were developing an underlying structure, a consistent transparency of motive and voice in their public comments. "The blogosphere is developing into an extraordinarily civil and deferential culture. This evolution is being led by a small cadre of influencers who are setting behavioral standards of which Disraeli would have approved." Not all social networking in the business will meet the Disraeli standard, but much of it does.

Next Steps: Analytics and Business Intelligence

Another major use of computing power in business that will be furthered by adoption of the cloud is the use of analytical systems or business intelligence. When a project's information is located on a small set of similar servers, tapping into and analyzing that information will prove easier than if it is spread across incompatible systems. When a project's information is tied to product sales activity on the company Web site, and both are powered by the internal cloud, then that information can be analyzed and cross-referenced more easily than when it must be drawn from disparate systems. It has been nearly impossible to get real-time information on the business, even though good historical information is available through the process of data warehousing. New systems, such as complex event processing (CEP), can look at events in the software infrastructure, such as the removal of an item from inventory (an event in both the physical and digital worlds via the inventory system). CEP can gain an understanding of how fast certain events are occurring, the time frames in which they are occurring, the metrics that should be applied to determine whether they were outside a well-established norm, and so on. Complex event processing doesn't require the cloud, but it is one of those new software capabilities that will show unexpected analysis and insight emerging from cloud operations.

In short, in many organizations, IT is already charging itself to introduce "cloudlike" capabilities into the firm's data center operations, whether that direction has come from the top or not. At root, what's needed is not a particular type of computing so much as a platform for flexible business operations. This chapter projects that an internal cloud, working at times with external cloud resources, will be such a platform. It's a platform that can expand for certain users upon need and can support a high degree of social networking, information retrieval, and sharing. It goes without saying that a new company culture that understands the value of such collaborative computing devices is also needed.

A Glimpse of a Flexible, Cloud-Based Future

Let's consider a future scenario that perhaps illustrates how such a business culture could come about.

It had been known for some time that something was amiss in your company's industry. Competitors who had defended their turf for years seemed to be falling away overnight. Far from being reassured, your company's leaders were nervous that the same thing might also happen to your company.

One day, a sure sign of trouble loomed on the horizon. A new competitor in Malaysia had come up with an advanced design of your flagship product. The upstart didn't have the brand recognition that your company had, but it had had a string of previous successes that had overturned established players. Now months of bickering and indecision inside your company have to come to a head.

The leadership in IT had already started the process. It recognized that some form of cloud computing would be the business platform of the future and had started to reorganize. To get it right, however, it needed to know what the company's product strategy would be, and it had had little direction on that point. However, the CIO had tried to position IT as being ready to supply the tools and technologies that would allow the company to seize the initiative when the need arose. Now it had arrived—in the form of an unwelcome new competitor.

A mid-level manager in manufacturing had been talking outside of channels to his counterparts in research, design, and engineering. The young manager had also been out to talk to customers about your latest product and gotten an earful of bad feedback on its design and functionality.

On the company Web site, senior design managers had put forth their best ideas in a forum, but, to their frustration, they had been shot down by the new president of the customer user group. He lacked the courtly manners of his predecessor and seemed to think that every opinion he held was right. Senior design management was offended.

On the other hand, hidden in his comments was the germ of an idea that even the new competition hadn't figured out. Instead of sticking with their favorite notions, some designers had consulted research on whether a new product could be executed with new materials. The answer to a key question was maybe. But it was too late for that. The young turk in manufacturing had seen enough and openly called for a new product design, with specifications to be delivered to manufacturing in record time. He had no authority to do this, but everyone knew that he was right to demand action.

In an unusual move, the manufacturing manager, formerly derided as "a nuts and bolts guy," was named as the head of a new product design team. He immediately insisted that two peers in other parts of the organization, over whom he had no authority, were indispensable members of the team. They were coworkers with whom he had been engaged in the background debate. The CEO approved the nominations. Out of the shadows stepped what amounted to a multimember, cross-disciplinary team of planners, designers, marketers, and engineers who had been watching the company's inaction with growing alarm.

This team was self-selected, based on a web of invisible contacts and personal networking, but now its shadow organization had to become explicit. IT's advance work in implementing cloud computing as a business platform was about to pay off. The team self-provisioned several virtual servers, one to serve as a wiki, an e-mail aggregation server, a "who we are" team biography Web page, and a Web portal with various software tools for blogging and building a library of references and documents. Each member was given a blog on which to post his measure of progress once a day, and also air criticisms of and support for other members of the team. There were no rules governing this discourse other than that it had to be direct, it had to be transparent (no hidden agendas), and it could not become personal. As long as someone is commenting on the issues at hand, criticism is fair comment until the group decides otherwise. It would collectively note any tendency by certain team members to get too competitive with a fellow team member; in fact, it was ready to reprimand such conduct. But there was little of that. The team had selected itself based on respect for the core leadership. Some of the commentaries and exchanges got a little rough, but it was simply understood: you will contribute your best opinions and defend them or be replaced by someone who will.

Additional virtual servers hosted product data, a recruiting site where team members talked about previous projects they'd worked on and people they'd worked with, including those at other companies. They frankly discussed possible additional members and recruited targeted employees. On the wiki, the discussion turned to what team members wished they knew but didn't. A marketer attempted to design clever questions and insert them into customer forums, but they drew little response. Then the team leader adopted a controversial stance on where the product ought to go and customer comment flooded in, some of it bitingly critical: "Even if you could build such a thing, what makes you think your technical support could understand it?" However, a surprising amount of the comment was positive.

It had been only two weeks, but all the working facilities had been set up, a rudimentary product design drawn, and a direction achieved. A prototype was being attempted in the lab. Meanwhile, comments were flying back and forth on why relying so much on new components and subassemblies would drive the project asunder versus why proven components were simply not up to the job.

All was going well until someone pointed out that a key existing subassembly was in short supply and there was no second source. The best brains in manufacturing were brought in, but no solution suggested itself other than to redesign the prototype. No one wanted to do that at such a late date, so the team leader turned to his ring of personal acquaintances on LinkedIn, seeking a reference to a young, eager company that could be trained in the work of building a new subassembly. A strong candidate emerged from the process.

An additional collaboration site was set up in an external cloud so that engineers at the new subassembly maker could talk with engineers at the manufacturer. The project leader at the new supplier even had access to the manufacturer's internal cloud sites. In fact, several additional virtual machines had been provisioned by the project team, and three of them were sitting idle, wasting resources. In a routine sweep, IT discovered their lack of activity in the fourth week and decommissioned them, with the project team's permission. The team leader attributed the overprovisioning to the overzealousness of certain valued team members.

The product was launched on time to head off the competition, and customers were impressed by what it could do. Three months after the launch, the company Web site suddenly experienced a rush of product information requests along with increased purchase activity. Minute analysis of click-through activity on the site showed that many of the competitor's customers had come to the established manufacturer's site to look for the product, but they were using keywords that were not part of your company's background or culture. The site was redesigned to build in references to these keywords and the process they represent. A new segment of customers had been found and traffic on the site again increased, pushing its ability to complete transactions. But this issue had been foreseen. Part of the traffic was shunted off to a backup Web site in a public cloud, where searches could be conducted and read-only information was dispensed. With a multichannel approach, the new product launch was a success and your company learned the value of the cloud.

That's a rough scenario of how a company met a challenge. Throughout, it should be clear that it succeeded not because it was well prepared, but in spite of being ill prepared. It had a rudimentary internal cloud in place to supply the means for a flexible organization to launch once the challenge was clearly defined. It immediately started to make use of a previously troublesome and disregarded customer feedback loop. It started putting social networking to work, not just playing on Facebook. The cloud's ability to host many forms of collaboration allowed the project to move forward quickly.

In any scenario, cloud computing is going to fall short of solving all problems. Human ingenuity will still be the ultimate requirement in meeting the challenges. But putting in place the right training, the right tools, and the right platform for problem solving can make the difference between survival and going out of business.

(((**10**)))

CALCULATING
THE FUTURE

Shorter lines of communication, deeper background relationships between employees, and more shared knowledge of
the company up and down the ranks—that's a reorganized
business, one that is better able to cope with the changes that
are sure to come its way.

Cloud computing isn't required if a company is to accomplish all this but it's an enabler of much of it. And if it works
that way inside the company, why can't the cloud do something similar for those important relationships outside the
company, especially that key one between the company and
its customers? In fact, when the cloud is used along with other
initiatives, it can do just that.

Business management is always seeking a better way to capture customer loyalty. In the past, that has meant selling something that the customer needed, but including a hook in the product or service that more or less involuntarily tied the customer to the company. As long as he is using the product, he has to keep coming back. Printers need ink cartridges just as razors need blades. It's not a new story.

But the current climate is different from what has gone before. Business managers are trying to fight their way out of a deep recession. Wary customers are still reluctant to spend. What's the formula for success in such a setting? Just as cloud computing can reshape relationships inside the company, it can provide a platform for relating to customers in a whole new way—a way that can perhaps take into account a certain unease with the straitened circumstances in which many of those customers find themselves. As businesses attempt to recover from the downturn, they will not only be competing with rivals for revenue, but also struggling to restore trust to customer relationships. That trust may have been frayed by hard times, if not irritation, anger, and impatience with Wall Street's business-as-usual crowd that helped bring on a risk-filled recession in the first place.

If social networking, wikis, blogging, and community forums ease communication inside the company, why can't the company use the same platform to put its best foot forward with customers? Why can't it display its core competencies and primary values in every interaction with the customer, strengthening the relationship?

Under the cloud computing model, customers can come to the company's Web site not only to view information, but also to activate services in which the company gives away something that illustrates its core competence and passion for a subject area. The information or service used to be bundled into a product with a price tag. Now the customer is impressed with what the company can do for him before he's spent a dollar. Finding such an extended hand useful, the customer comes back for more and finds that the company has a list of services that the customer can activate, order to do certain things, and control. The customer can designate services and use them as tools to build a custom product—a special piece of outdoor gear, a compost machine that fits into a corner of the basement, or a business service that combines what were previously separate services into one. In the future, all these things might be possible because the cloud can host sophisticated software that has incorporated business rules, professional knowledge, and even specialized knowledge, such as a complex chemical process, and can use them to build a sophisticated product or service. And at the same time, the software can be activated and manipulated by a remote end user employing a home PC or an even simpler computing device. The control will be extended to the user by building simple user interfaces in front of the complex computing system. With "programmatic control" over how services are manipulated, the customer can direct the software services to do things and be dazzled by the amount of expertise that's been handed off to him. And such a customer will keep coming back for more.

At the same time, this new business platform is capturing more customer data through the interactions that are going on in the cloud. It can make that data available to customer sales and service representatives in close to real time—as it happens. When it seems appropriate, a sales representative might jump in and point out things that can be done that the customer appears to be interested in doing. No longer does the customer have to go to the store to have an encounter with a knowledgeable floor salesperson. It's all available online. And the software events created through all these interactions contain clues to what the customer is looking for and what he's likely to be willing to pay for.

The Cloud Sets Off a New, Disruptive Way of Doing Things

It wasn't so long ago that Tim Berners-Lee enhanced the Internet with a few simple conventions that let documents be posted, linked to, and read remotely. The first phase of the Web was one of read-only information, and while businesses could adopt it as an additional communication medium, that advantage was spread around fairly evenly and disruption of established businesses was minimal.

The second phase of the Web was the distribution of information plus narrowly defined services. It was characterized by simple interactions, and it limited computing by the end user, which usually amounted to making a few entries in a form in a browser window. Some industry segments were disrupted, and a few new super-services, such as the search engine, music downloading, travel, and Webmail, emerged, buttressing the fortunes of a few companies. A share of consumer retailing moved online. The book distribution/selling business was disrupted, and online auctions and trading platforms became a new medium of exchange. Middlemen, information gatekeepers of all sorts, were replaced by the interactive information delivery mechanisms of the Web.

Cloud computing represents a third and more disruptive phase of Internet computing. This phase consists of information plus broad services and products. It is characterized by deeper interactions powered by unlimited peer-to-peer-style computing, where each party may vary or build out the exchange. The meaning of the end user gaining programmatic control is that, in some instances, the interaction can go as far as both parties want it to rather than only as far as one party restricted it. The nature of the interaction can change as it occurs. The data center can present the end user with new options geared to a particular individual that it seems to recognize. The end user can send back to the data center modified software that tells it where she wants to go. In phase three, a narrow service can be followed by another that was specifically requested by the end user, then by one that was co-built with the end user. The cloud rolls up the changes of the first two phases and combines them with a powerful engine to do much more in this third phase. In this sense, the cloud computing phase is more likely to undermine established businesses than its predecessors. It promises to be a broadly disruptive technology wave, changing the way companies relate to their customers. As it matures over the next few years, unease with the term *cloud computing* will disappear, and this disruption will become known as the cloud revolution.

To Disrupt or Be Disrupted

What generally happens to businesses when they are faced with disruptive change? A number of fascinating studies have captured the effects of disruption. In summary, they say that a new, low-cost way of doing things appears, based on new technology underpinnings. Initially, established businesses reject the change because it isn't as well developed as the products they offer. It also lowers prices and margins and is unsuitable for their core customer base. The early adopters are not their customers anyway, and they represent low-profit prospects. The change, however, is revised, improved upon, and built out by those who see value in it, and it is adopted by more and more customers. Established businesses see their customers starting to make a shift, so they rush into the new technology. But leadership in the segment has already been assumed by those who pioneered its development. Established businesses decline or fail in the face of this new competition.

A book that graphically captures the sequence and draws measured conclusions from it is *The Innovator's Dilemma*, by Clayton M. Christensen (HarperBusiness, 2000). Established businesses have a hard time coping with disruptive change because their culture has set up processes and cultivated patterns of thought that serve their existing customers. To serve customers in an emerging market, it's necessary to take a few people out of that culture, allow them to assess the change, and reward them based on their ability to exploit it. In my simplistic synopsis, this subunit of the company will grow with the use of the disruptive technology and teach the parent organization, when the time comes, how to cope. Companies that do this, or some variation of it, such as acquiring a technology leader that's at the heart of the change, may easily adapt to disruptive change. Then again, they may not. Think of Digital Equipment Corp. inventing the brilliant AltaVista search engine as a showcase for its Alpha servers, followed by the company's demise not long after, and it's hard to be optimistic.

How is cloud computing a disruptive change? The cloud certainly matches up with Christensen's criterion of a low-cost alternative that is seized upon by emerging markets, but maintained at arms length by established companies. It's often not immediately clear what is supposed to be done with disruptive technologies, since they don't seem to serve powerful existing buyers, another apt descriptor of the cloud.

Yet new uses emerge out of nowhere. For example, Facebook social networking is familiar enough and is even being used by large enterprises to encourage networks among their employees. But since June 2009, 63 million people have started using FarmVille, a Facebook application where they grow digital crops and manage virtual fields in a system that rewards them for good methods and punishes them for neglect. If there is a hidden desire to grow food and husband resources in our society, then FarmVille may be one of the few expressions of it. Facebook has had to expand its cloud data centers to support this activity. It's not clear how the free FarmVille users make any money for Facebook, but Facebook seems to be satisfied with its ability to garner millions of new users. Facebook may never monetize those 63 million users, but at least it has the option of trying to do so. Is it possible that seed and garden suppliers might want to advertise on FarmVille? Many businesses would like to have this problem, which Facebook has so effortlessly assimilated.

The cloud is disruptive in other ways as well. While a mainframe or a large Unix cluster was previously a difficult resource to access, the cloud makes great bursts of power—say, grabbing the services of 12 servers for two hours—relatively cheap. In the past, credentials as a researcher or a specialized business user were needed to access either enterprise or research center high-performance computing. The cloud makes it available to any taker who is willing to use a credit card.

A researcher used to spend months or years learning a computer language and building a program that could execute against the data that his project possessed. With aids in the cloud to build programs that will run in the cloud, this process can be simplified, extended to more people, and speeded up. A researcher will be able to count on the strength of the platform to provide some of the most complicated parts of the program, such as linking to a powerful database or moving data from storage to server memory caches at the right instant. The researcher won't have to produce all the code to do this himself.

Microsoft and IBM are about to supply cloud frameworks based on their development tools; they will illustrate how the environment in which you develop aids deployment. Salesforce .com has been and remains a pioneer in this space, constantly expanding the tools that a customer can use to enlarge an existing Salesforce application or build a new one for the Force .com platform. Fewer and fewer specialized skills are needed to construct a cloud application. Software that exists in the cloud helps build software to be run there.

In addition, cloud development will extend programming skills to many new participants because the platform itself can invoke many automated steps in the process. The tools used will be simplified, and in some cases users will be given a checklist of choices, unfolding in a carefully planned sequence, that will allow nearly anyone to build simple software applications, then run them.

How will such a resource be used? Well, as Christensen observes, "Disruptive technologies often enable something to be done that previously had been deemed impossible." In the face of a disruptive technology, he urges "agnostic marketing." No one, neither supplier nor consumer, is sure how or in what quantities a new product or resource will be used. So don't assume that you know. Find a way to experiment with the customer.

"Markets for disruptive technologies often emerge from unanticipated successes. . . . Discoveries often come by watching how people use products rather than by listening to what they say." In other words, the new markets are discovered, not by focus groups of existing customers who may not even be familiar with a disruptive technology, but by those who use it directly. In many cases, there will even be a generation split as younger people take to the disruptive technology and implement it, while their elders hold back, satisfied that what they've got is good enough.

"Discovering markets for emerging technologies inherently involves failure, and most individual decision makers find it very difficult to risk backing a project that might fail because the market is not there," Christiansen warns, and you begin to see why the disruptive technology creeps up on so many companies unawares.

Smart people are already seizing on the possibilities of cloud computing and putting it to use in ways that many established businesses can't foresee. Passionate individuals who suddenly realize that the cloud provides them with an avenue to do something that they've always wanted to do—research a problem, assemble a team, or produce a service—will find ways to do it in the cloud. Small companies with an instinct for what can be done and a knack for creating a profitable cloud service will find venture capital backing.

Tomorrow's Scenarios

As this is being written, Amazon's Elastic Compute Cloud (EC2) is three years old and rapidly maturing. In the midst of a severe recession, not everybody is paying attention. Cutting costs has been the mentality that has dominated the landscape for the last two years and may continue to assert itself deep into 2010. Perhaps some companies will start to consider the possibilities of cloud computing as the economy revives.

Meanwhile, those people who are left running computers and manning consoles at many companies have little time for experimenting or considering the implications of the cloud. For many, its impact won't be realized until long after its early adopters have had a long head start.

Consider the following possible example of the type of disruptive change that will be flowing through the economy soon.

You first noticed a change when a large home builder in your community went out of business. He hadn't noticed the start-up firms that based their business on allowing prospective owners to design their own homes. Prospects were given a system on which they built a design, with the price required to produce the design guaranteed by the builder. The large home builder had a few floor plans that had proved popular over the years. The little firms offered an architect on a USB device, with thousands of features and floor plans. The system on its own constantly consulted materials pricing and expertise on the Internet, then assimilated new options into the design choices. One person designed a house with energy-saving appliance management features and a solar panel roof. Another installed a space where an older relative could have some privacy. Another, a gardener, installed gray-water diversion plumbing for watering plants without violating his household's water quota. Some wanted a wine cellar; others, a continuous wireless network. The skilled but traditional builder had heard of such things but had rejected them as too expensive and requiring expertise beyond the limits of his firm. And as these wacky designs came off the printer, the houses were being built with only the design firm serving as the general contractor. Each design firm used an alliance of small builders, a set of specialists assembled ad hoc to produce a particular house. The traditional builder hadn't noticed this reorganization of skills in his industry. It seemed to occur overnight, although some of his own crew had drifted away to join these outfits. As house after house went up, he asked around; no one knew of an architect, mortgage broker, Realtor, or lawyer who had been involved in any of the projects, but many people had heard details about the homes' unique, owner-inspired details.

These changes had been abrupt enough, but the most shocking was the decline in the workload of the aerospace engineer up the street. He had been overworked for three years straight as his firm struggled to bring a bigger, more cost-efficient airliner off the drawing boards. In addition to design, the firm had to implement a worldwide supply chain of sub-assembly suppliers and bring the parts together in its own plant. The project in fact had gone well, and the jets were beginning to come off the assembly line, although they were years behind their scheduled profits. The company also had several smaller projects under way. It needed new markets to keep its revenues healthy and its staff fully employed. It had tried smaller craft and even an experimental pilotless plane that could carry overnight packages. But it had totally missed what proved to be the best new market for the industry in 50 years—space travel. Everyone in the industry knew that space flight was not part of the friendly skies. It was something that required a big government agency working with defense industry rocket makers. No one had sensed how much the new composite materials could shrink the weight and size of a stubby-winged, clamshell aircraft that could take off, stage a shallow climb to 130,000 feet over 48 hours, and from there convert a jet engine into a rocket motor for blastoff into space. Once in space, the vehicle used the moon and earth's gravity to whip it around and send it on its return trip, just like the antique Apollo space capsules had done. Being able to say that you'd seen the dark side of the moon seemed to make the $7,349 price of a ticket worth it, and the spacecraft's makers even had the nerve to say that the carbon footprint of the trip was no greater than that of a regular passenger's flight from Los Angeles to New York. How could that be? The aerospace engineer said that it would have taken platoons of engineers and several billion dollars to come up with the design of the tourist spacecraft at his company, but somehow OuterAdventures Inc. had done it. Now all that the airlines were interested in was building up their fleets of clamshell spacecraft. How had his firm missed this market? He was employed only part time and was trying to find someone who was interested in his jet airplane design skills.

This same story was repeated in many forms over and over again until it was clear that a broad disruption was sweeping through much of the economy. No one could point a finger at a single cause, but many industry segments were undergoing rapid change. One thing was clear. Many of the parties that were driving the changes were using the cloud, but you were never sure exactly how they were using it. Sometime around EC2's fifth birthday, the self-provisioning end user and the cloud data center seemed to mesh into one ongoing, disruptive force.

The scenarios given here are fanciful, but I'm not so sure that they will be a few years from now. Companies must decide whether they are going to sit passively and watch a wave of disruption wash over their operations or harness the power of the cloud for themselves.

Harnessing the Cloud

A wise manager can invoke one of several strategies to cope with the impending changes; no single strategy is going to be right for all companies. But last-minute demands that things must change is not the right approach. Employees who believe that they are doing a good job by executing the company's long-held tenets need a road map to guide them along the correct lines of what to do next.

Within any organization, however, there may be two or three strong performers or a small team that has an interest in cloud computing. Ask these people to form an informal group that will draw up a list of ways in which the company is most likely to be affected by the cloud and another list of what the company might do in the cloud. At first, this may be a barren exercise, executed by people who think that their existing responsibilities give them plenty to do. But it signals to everyone that the company is interested. It may bring forth good ideas from the parties who are assigned the responsibility, as they think about it against the background of what they do, or from someone unnamed who has his own grasp of what the cloud can do and sees that the company is interested in learning about cloud computing. Many short-staffed firms might name a computer professional to such a task, but it's important that someone with a keen understanding of the business be involved as well. Such a person would soon see that some customer-related business processes can be executed more effectively in the cloud.

In larger organizations, an IT professional or a small team of them with a knack for talking to the business analysts and managers might experiment with sending workloads to the cloud to learn how it's done and map out which types of work might be offloaded there. Beyond that, it would be possible to build prototype services in the cloud to illustrate what the company could do for customers if it wished to use the cloud as more than a laboratory.

An immediate avenue worth exploring would be whether customer communities might be formed that could provide valuable feedback to the company. The Web site manager might argue that his domain is the proper one for such a community, and in many cases, it would be. But a community that is functioning in the cloud would have the option for customer interactions beyond those on the Web site. It could give customers "programmatic control" over code options that the company makes available or accept customer code to see if it would work with existing services. Software tools could be put into the hands of customers to make greater use of existing services or co-build new ones. Trying to do so on servers inside the corporate firewall might open up the company to a security breach. Trying to do so on the Web site might disrupt the site or bring it down. But doing so in a virtual machine in the cloud keeps production systems free from the vicissitudes of end user experimentation. Other customers might join in at a community site. In the middle of the night, two customers who couldn't resist trying one more thing might collaborate in staging a breakthrough.

With a disruption, remember, neither the consumer nor the company knows exactly how the disruptive technology might be used. Giving the customer programmatic control over certain resources produced by the company is commonplace at companies like Microsoft, IBM, Google, and Salesforce.com. But many established companies are unfamiliar with how the practice works (the controls have strict limits) or how it might be employed safely to work for them. Services today are built in software, and software as a service in the cloud is a new distribution method and economic model. Salesforce.com has grown quickly and has proved that this technique works.

If early feedback makes any of these avenues appear promising, the company might take Christensen's advice and create a small unit with no responsibility other than to try to exploit the new opening, with any returns applauded, whether they contribute significantly to overall profits or not. If neither that unit nor the competition gets anywhere with one avenue of exploration, it can be abandoned without too much upheaval. If, after a couple of failures, an avenue points the way to success, the company will have ready-made expertise in its ranks and will have made a wise investment.

Nor will success with the cloud necessarily come from the appointed team. Some line-of-business manager that you didn't know had any programming skills may learn enough PHP to use the cloud to design a new process or product without anyone realizing it—a kind of cloud skunk works. Top management will have to decide whether such behavior gets rewarded or punished, but when it comes to disruptive change, the more direct experimentation with a disruptive wave, the better. In all likelihood, after his innovation is adopted, the line-of-business manager will be admonished to stick to the proven methods of the company. If he keeps his nerve, exercises his ability to invoke cloud computing again, and succeeds a second time, narrowly beating out the competition, he will go from dog to hero. Through frequent iterations of the software features on the new product, the company pulls ahead. The cost of experimentation in the cloud will be slight compared to the cost of unfettered competition emerging in a field that you know nothing about.

"Programmatic Control" Means That the Customer Takes Charge

We emphasized the potential of small firms using the cloud for advanced design because designing a product in advance of a market has usually been impossible in the past. The design process is too expensive to be attempted willy-nilly without an identifiable market. The scenarios given previously postulate that design might shift out of the conventional sequence in producing products in a cloud disruption. Once a market is identified and customers are consulted, design on expensive in-house CAD/CAM systems usually follows. But a cloud could serve as a low-cost design platform. Instead of equipping highly paid designers, customers might come to the cloud and use advanced software design systems that are resident there. The software would incorporate the rules and regulations and best practices of, say, building a house, and allow the user to try to design a highly customized model without an architect looking over her shoulder. Then a specialist product management firm would figure out how to produce the product. Instead of trying to sell something to people who don't necessarily want it, you've enlisted potential customers to design something that they're willing to pay for. Perhaps a business gains only a few customers from such a process, but it has still gathered a core of paying customers, plus a mother lode of information on what your potential customers are interested in—free market research.

A cloud computing platform can also serve as a staging ground for a marketplace, with talented outsiders being brought into the market for periodic contributions through a screening process. A variety of market transactions take place in this vertical cloud, because the independent companies are united in their goals, but not in their corporate structure. The wide-ranging group doesn't need to be inside the same company because all financial transactions take place in the shared cloud infrastructure and are auditable there. We are rapidly moving toward being able to monitor, audit, and manage all events in a given software infrastructure, if we choose to do so.

For example, the day may come when government regulators make all mortgage lending take place within a vertical "mortgage cloud" where each step of the process could be audited down to the point of identifying who said that a mortgage applicant had sufficient income for the mortgage. Another round of bad mortgage creation and reselling like the last one might bring about such a "regulatory" cloud. At any time they choose, government auditors can move in and reconstruct the events that led to the issuing of an unsound mortgage or set of mortgages, based upon falsified income information and other misleading statements. In the not-so-distant past, such mortgages were common, but when they are discovered only in retrospect, it's difficult to tell who made what decision where in the falsification process. Not that there was any zeal expressed on the part of regulators. In the mortgage cloud, all decisions are auditable and reconstructable from their software events, and those who were responsible for each event have been required to leave a digital signature on it. Imagine the impact on the trustworthiness of mortgages. And if it brings economic rationality and accountability to this reckless group, then it may allow free association of responsible individuals into a shared marketplace where you bid your services and receive your (auditable) rewards. Auditable cloud computing transactions might one day change or even replace some corporate structures. Software interactions are events that can now be identified, tracked, and reconstructed at will.

During disruptive change, products will anticipate markets rather than waiting for them to emerge in concrete form. To do so "will entail a process of mutual discovery by customers and manufacturers," writes Christensen. One of the few ways in which this can come about is if companies form communities with their customers, giving them free expertise and services on top of the products they sell, and listening to their feedback. The model for such communities is the open source code project, where a core of skilled developers contributes code and manages a product, while a much larger community of users contributes additional code when it can and tests the code that the core developers say is ready for use. The lines of communication are short and direct; the code's the thing, and someone who is skilled at electronic interactions cultivates the community and listens to its feedback. If companies had communities of users instead of "customer bases," they would multiply the channels for feedback and build that feedback into their product specification and design processes.

Whatever your strategy may be, it must recognize that the cloud is going to serve as an ongoing, democratizing force, putting more computer power into the hands of all kinds of end users and delivering more expertise and services to them. The cloud will share many kinds of professional intelligence in specialized fields with the masses, and in some cases, individual recipients are going to augment that intelligence with their own.

The cloud is a continuation of the original end user revolt against centralized computing and the master/slave relationship. Now end users have their own computers, and they are rapidly changing their capabilities and form. They have come to realize that carrying your own computer with you is not the only way to take charge of your computing needs. The services of a powerful networked data center can greatly augment whatever your personal machine can do, especially when as many resources as needed can be summoned out of the data center. As these two forces interact—an intelligent end user on one end and a powerful data center on the other—a new world will emerge, dissimilar to the one that preceded it. Digital culture will be with us from the moment we wake up until the moment we go to bed. The greatest achievements of the human race will be immediately with us, to the point of participation.

How are we going to adapt to this envelope of digital culture and the cloud that supplies it? While it has the capability for misuse, it also promises to collapse the distances between groups that are interested in working together and between people who are discovering each other's special characteristics and unique heritage. It gives the inquisitive and adventurous in different societies the prospect of combining skills in new and unexpected ways.

As a business platform, the cloud offers a 24-hours-a-day business presence, displaying the knowledge and expertise about which the business is passionate and establishing interactive communities around that expertise. The company's customers will share their knowledge with one another, and in the process provide clues about the direction in which the business needs to go. Through greater collaboration, the business can select leaders from within its customers' ranks, displaying their accomplishments as part of its own and building a wider sense of community in a mutual, ongoing endeavor. By giving customers a two-way channel through which they may both speak and act, the business will gain invaluable insight into who its customers are, where their interests lie, and what it might do next to meet their anticipated needs. Design teams with no customers on them will become a thing of the past.

This, then, is the cloud revolution: a tenfold gain in economies of scale, a similar multiplier of end users' compute power, and an increase in businesses' ability to relate to customers. It is also a potentially disruptive force that is about to wash through many industry segments. Within the cloud platform lies the ability for newcomers to create level playing fields and ethical transaction exchanges where they will fight for position among established players. Will cloud computing lead to your company's success—or something else? The answer lies in the hands of those who understand this revolution, seize the resource, and go to work with it.

NEBULA: NASA'S STRATEGIC CLOUD

The federal government wants to reduce the heterogeneous nature of federal data centers by figuring out a way to build them to a more common standard and reduce the burgeoning expense of IT for U.S. citizens. There's early evidence that the government thinks that cloud computing is part of the answer.

Like that of the modern business world, the government's appetite for computing power keeps growing, and the number and types of data centers are increasing along with it. NASA has been a target of critics who say that federal agencies spend too much on information technology and create too many computing centers. NASA, with its Houston Space Flight Center, Cape Kennedy launch site, Jet Propulsion Lab in Pasadena, California, and Goddard Space Flight Center in Greenbelt, Maryland, among other branches, has a need for shareable resources that can be easily accessed by employees in locations other than the one in which the data center was built. In that sense, NASA has sometimes served as a symbol for the federal government as a whole, where the number of data centers has proliferated, growing from 498 centers 10 years ago to more than 1,200 today.

The federal government now spends $76 billion a year on information technology, and Vivek Kundra, the first chief information officer overseeing all federal data centers, appointed in 2009 by President Barack Obama, has endorsed the concept of cloud computing as one way to bring escalating costs under control.

Kundra made a splash in September 2009 when he launched apps.gov, a simple marketplace and rudimentary form of cloud computing where federal agencies can go to buy software. But another project has been proceeding behind the scenes for the last 18 months, one whose long-term goals are more ambitious than those of apps.gov: the Nebula Cloud Computing Platform. The Nebula Cloud Computing Platform is being worked on at the same site where Kundra announced apps.gov, the NASA Ames Research Center in Mountain View, California.

Kundra has made only a few short references to Nebula— it's still in an experimental stage—but few doubt that his and other federal officials' hopes are riding on it beyond the scant mention that it has received. NASA in particular has a number of strategic goals riding on the Nebula project, goals that are distinct from but not terribly different from those of many businesses. They include

- Finding a model for an easy-to-construct data center that can be put to flexible use

- Having such a data center incorporate the latest economies of scale

- Making the data center easy to expand

- Making it a resource that can be shared with other agencies

- Furthering public engagement with NASA

- Offering a platform based on open source code

- Contributing NASA-produced code as open source code that other agencies will be able to use

- Making the data center easy to virtualize and manage

- Making it easier for researchers and partners outside of NASA to use NASA's data and computing facilities

Nebula has several factors working in its favor. It is being built at a federal research center that was an early participant in ARPAnet, which later became the Internet. It also sits at the location of the MAE-West, a major hub for top-flight Internet service providers as well as the location of one of the servers of the Domain Name System, a set of servers that translate Web browser entries in an English language URL into a specific Transmission Control Protocol/Internet Protocol (TCP/IP) address on the Internet. An estimated $3 billion in capital equipment is in use at Ames, where 2,300 researchers are at work, with a high percentage of them having advanced computer skills. In short, as a result of its location and culture, Ames has an atmosphere of constant experiment and development related to the Internet.

NASA has stated that it wants to use the Ames Nebula Cloud Computing Platform as a means of reengaging the public's interest in NASA's space exploration, no simple task after the highs achieved by the breathtaking Apollo missions to the moon and the Rover missions that laid bare some of the secrets of Mars' red landscape. The Ames Research Center's early attempts at citizen involvement might serve as an example for what businesses could do if they decided to invoke the resources of a similar cloud platform.

First of all, let's describe what has happened so far with Nebula.

The Nebula platform is the future host for many NASA Web sites, once its management software is ready for the task. Nebula hosts the Web site nebula.nasa.gov, which contains information, blogs, and reader comments about the Nebula cloud resource. But Nebula is still a prototype, a work in progress; at the time of this writing, it is expected to be available in beta operational mode in March 2010. It is intended to host more Web sites at a lower cost than the present method of building them.

William Fellows, cloud analyst at the 451 Group, wrote in a December 10, 2009, report, "NASA Seeks Cloud Benefits Using

Open Source Nebula," that the space agency "spends far too much on IT. Each NASA group typically builds its own data center, and procurement can take as long as 40 weeks for a Web site. Nebula aims to reduce this time to a few minutes."

NASA reportedly hosts 3,000 internal and external Web sites today in its various data centers; the federal government as a whole has 100,000 Web sites. What would be the savings if they and future NASA Web sites could all be hosted in the Nebula cloud? In an update on the situation, NASA spokespersons say that a small staff of trained Web site developers could maintain many different Web sites built in a shared infrastructure, such as Nebula. That's impossible as long as each NASA agency has its own data center and its own Web site staff doing things in its own unique way.

Although software is still being written for the site, Nebula has made extensive use of freely available open source code. It includes the Linux operating system and the Linux cluster file system, Lustre File System, from Sun Microsystems, which is used by 15 of the largest supercomputing clusters in the world and is designed to work across thousands of servers in a single cluster. Nebula also uses the Django Web application framework, a tool for rapid building of lightweight Python scripting language Web applications, and Solr, an open source indexing and search engine.

One of its key components is the open source Eucalyptus Project's cloud application programming interfaces (APIs), which mimic the basic functions of Amazon Web Services' Elastic Compute Cloud (EC2). Because of that, "all Amazon

Web Services-compatible tools will work 'out-of-the-box' or with minor customization" for building and tweaking applications designed for Nebula, according to information posted on the Nebula Web site, nebula.nasa.gov. Virtual machines designed to run in Nebula under the open source Xen or KVM hypervisors can also be run in Amazon's EC2, giving NASA teams or NASA's partners and research collaborators an alternative site to run their applications. "By adopting Eucalyptus, we've bootstrapped the Nebula ecosystem with tools and systems that were made for EC2 and will make many available for you to use with Nebula," wrote JLindsay, an Ames Research Center staffer working on Nebula, in a blog, "How Eucalyptus Enables EC2 Compatibility with Nebula," on November 16, 2009.

In short, Nebula developers have taken advantage of the Amazon example and made use of an approach to cloud computing that offers flexibility for the future. The open source code is proven high-quality code and a way to avoid commercial software license expenses. It's also a shortcut to implementing cloud computing goals. NASA Ames staffers will produce more code to tie disparate open source code together and gain greater integration. The results of the Ames staffers' efforts will also be made open source code at some point in the future.

"NASA specific additions will be given back to the open source community. Nebula is intended to be a 'good example' of a successful large-scale open source project in the government and pave the way for similar project in other agencies,"

JLindsay wrote in the November 16, 2009, blog. This is a strategic goal of NASA: increasing its participation in open source projects and reaping the benefit of more open source developers being involved in reviewing and testing the code it produces.

"The ease of being able to pluck computing power out of the cloud will make a lot of new technologies more accessible. Free and open source software will hopefully be a big part of an efficient, transparent and cloud-empowered government," JLindsay concluded. The assumption is that open source development activity focused on one federal cloud will be easily transferred to other federal clouds, if it is decided that more data centers will be built on the cloud pattern. Such an approach would have the effect of standardizing the software in the data centers and lowering their cost.

According to information posted on the Nebula Web site, "the platform itself will help facilitate the adoption of open source software across the Government. Because of the ease of spinning up virtual machines and having a library of pre-made machine images, almost anybody (whether in IT or not) can set themselves up with an environment in which to test open source solutions in just a few minutes. This lowers the barrier to entry for trying new software, eliminating the downloading, installing and configuring, and providing a temporary test bed for experimentation and evaluation."

The Nebula cloud software is being written to run on Nebula's containerized x86 data center servers. The Ames Research Center last year received delivery of a 40-foot Verari

FOREST Container packed with x86 servers. Verari designs the power and cooling features and rack layout in its FOREST containers. Not a lot has been published about the exact design of the servers, other than to say that some were produced by NASA Ames's Silicon Valley neighbor, Cisco Systems, which was clearly looking for a marquee customer for its new Unified Computing System servers. Cisco entered the market for virtualized blade servers in the summer of 2009. A second supplier was Silicon Mechanics, a Bothell, Washington, supplier of rack mount servers designed for virtualization and cluster computing.

Buying servers in a container shipping unit means that NASA Ames doesn't need to plan a construction site two years in advance or build a building with a raised data center floor. According to Dell, which is also in the business of packing shipping containers with servers, a unit can be ordered, built, and delivered in 90 days.

NASA Ames CIO Chris Kemp hasn't commented on the specifics of the servers, but he says that the plug-in, shipping container format suits NASA's goals. In an interview with *InformationWeek*'s Nick Hoover, Kemp said that he plans to add more containers with the goal of moving them around. "The container model is great because we can move them wherever we need them," he said. ("NASA Launches Portable Cloud Effort," December 17, 2009.)

NASA, for example, will be able to place containers at universities collaborating with the agency on space research or even at launch sites. Containers will be able to be moved around and plugged in, like those delivered by truck, and deposited on the concrete floor of Microsoft's Chicago cloud data center.

Nebula has already been used in one public engagement project. The Lunar Crater Observation and Sensing Satellite (LCROSS) was launched by NASA on June 18, 2009, to orbit the moon and try to detect water in the form of ice in its polar regions or shadowed craters. On October 9, the upper stage of the Centaur rocket that launched LCROSS was intentionally crashed into a crater in the south polar region of the moon to see whether LCROSS instruments would detect any water vapor or particles in the ejecta plume created by the crash. The experiment was meant to gain visibility into one of the moon's permanently darkened spots that might hold more ice than previously known.

NASA published the 4:30 a.m. time and date of the crash and encouraged amateur astronomers to focus cameras and video recorders on the planned site to collect as much information on the plume as possible. On a Web site dubbed "Citizen Science," it urged owners of 10- to 12-inch telescopes to train their instruments on the south polar region of the moon and attempt to capture spectrographs, still images, and video of the Centaur impact.

"The LCROSS Mission will actively solicit images of the impact from the public. These images will provide a valuable addition to the archive of data chronicling the impact and its aftermath. This site will include a gallery of images received from both the public and professional communities," said NASA's Web site devoted to the mission at http://lcross.arc .nasa.gov/observation.htm.

The result was several high-resolution images of the impact captured by amateurs being uploaded to the Citizen Science Web site hosted by Nebula and put on display there for 30 days. NASA spokespersons said that the impact was not as visible to earth-based telescopes as had been expected, so the effort didn't result in a permanent display of amateur work, as had been hoped. Nevertheless, specialized instruments trained on the impact plume confirmed that water was present at levels found in the driest of earth's deserts. The LCROSS experiment also illustrated to NASA agencies that a resource for enlisting public participation in projects was available. Several groups inside the agency are exploring how Nebula can help them engage the public in their next project.

So far, many groups inside NASA have made use of Nebula. There have been about 800 requests for use of its computing infrastructure, NASA Ames Research spokespersons said in an update conversation at the start of 2010. It is intended for use by agencies outside NASA as well. It has been equipped with the software controls that allow authorized users from outside the agency to provision themselves with virtual servers when they need them. One outside federal agency, the U.S. Office of Management and Budget (OMB), is a regular user of the Nebula infrastructure, which has charge-back and billing systems in place to collect fees for the amount of server time used. The OMB use is apparently a pilot project intended to illustrate the availability of Nebula to other parts of the federal government. Spokespersons say that the flow of chargeback revenue is helping to fund the ongoing development of Nebula.

Many businesses would be happy to reach out to the digitally oriented younger generation and find a means of achieving greater engagement with their customers of all ages. To do so through an internal cloud in their own data center or a public cloud such as GoGrid, Joyent, or Rackspace might prove a cost-effective way of reaching the public. The use of Nebula by geographically dispersed NASA and government organizations is also a model for businesses.

At the same time, there is a major difference between NASA and the business world. Nebula has been designed to be more secure than many other government computing sites. Because it has one shared architecture, imposing security measures and keeping them up to date is easier than it is in a data center with multiple operating systems or even multiple releases of the same operating system and other software. This argument that a more uniform architecture can provide greater security can be made on behalf of EC2 and other cloud resources used by businesses.

In addition, the Nebula developers have been able to sidestep a common business security problem: how to control customer-related data, transaction information, and other private data. By design, NASA is putting in Nebula only information that by definition is public information. Its goal is to achieve greater transparency and sharing of the agency's information through the cloud.

"The only information being stored on Nebula is rated as publicly available data and is not currently intended to store sensitive information. Nebula was created to enable NASA to engage with the public more easily on the Web and to make

NASA's data sets available to the public," according to the Nebula Web site.

Nevertheless, NASA's Nebula illustrates how cloud computing can further a set of strategic goals that hitherto have been too expensive or too time-consuming for each data center in the agency to implement on its own.

The Nebula cloud, like most other cloud operations, enables user self-provisioning. It runs virtual machines that are the equivalent of Amazon Machine Images under the open source hypervisor Xen. As a matter of fact, one way to study how to establish an Amazon Web Services–compatible private cloud—that is, one in which applications and virtual machines will be interchangeable with Amazon's EC2—is to learn from NASA's example.

NASA's approach to cloud computing nevertheless ties the technology to the overall mission of the agency. NASA's Ames Research Center illustrates how it has linked certain activities to cloud computing and how it plans to use cloud computing to achieve certain strategic goals.

As Nebula is a work in progress, not enough is known about it to say that it offers a pattern that businesses can use to achieve their own strategic goals. It's not known, for example, how much management software NASA has had to write itself to use with Nebula open source code or whether it has enlisted commercial products. But if future reports make it clear that Nebula is being invoked as a successful example by other agencies of the federal government, many businesses could profit from studying its example. It will have set a pattern for a standardized, easy-to-manage data center built to take advantage of economies of scale. It will be available to NASA agencies and outsiders on a pay-as-you-go basis. Users will be able to self-provision virtual servers, and billing will be automatically applied to that use.

If these techniques lower the overall cost of IT for NASA, then cloud computing will have proved to be one of Vivek Kundra's few options for achieving these goals in a constrained economic climate. Such constraints are likely to be with both the federal government and business for a long time to come, leaving cloud computing with a tall order to fill.

NIST DEFINITION OF CLOUD COMPUTING

Note 1: Cloud computing is still an evolving paradigm. Its definitions, use cases, underlying technologies, issues, risks, and benefits will be refined in a spirited debate by the public and private sectors. These definitions, attributes, and characteristics will evolve and change over time (October 2009).

Note 2: The cloud computing industry represents a large ecosystem of many models, vendors, and market niches. This definition attempts to encompass all of the various cloud approaches.

National Institute of Standards and Technology, Information Technology Laboratory.

Definition of Cloud Computing

Cloud computing is a model for enabling convenient, on-demand network access to a shared pool of configurable computing resources (e.g., networks, servers, storage, applications, and services) that can be rapidly provisioned and released with minimal management effort or service provider interaction. This cloud model promotes availability and is composed of five essential characteristics, three service models, and four deployment models.

Essential Characteristics

On-demand self-service. A consumer can unilaterally provision computing capabilities, such as server time and network storage, as needed automatically without requiring human interaction with each service's provider.

Broad network access. Capabilities are available over the network and accessed through standard mechanisms that promote use by heterogeneous thin or thick client platforms (e.g., mobile phones, laptops, and PDAs).

Resource pooling. The provider's computing resources are pooled to serve multiple consumers using a multitenant model, with different physical and virtual resources dynamically assigned and reassigned according to consumer demand. There is a sense of location independence in that the customer generally has no control or knowledge over the exact location of the provided resources but may be able to specify location at a higher level of abstraction (e.g., country, state, or data center). Examples of resources include storage, processing, memory, network bandwidth, and virtual machines.

Rapid elasticity. Capabilities can be rapidly and elastically provisioned, in some cases automatically, to quickly scale out and rapidly released to quickly scale in. To the consumer, the capabilities available for provisioning often appear to be unlimited and can be purchased in any quantity at any time.

Measured service. Cloud systems automatically control and optimize resource use by leveraging a metering capability at some level of abstraction appropriate to the type of service (e.g., storage, processing, bandwidth, and active user accounts). Resource usage can be monitored, controlled, and reported providing transparency for both the provider and consumer of the utilized service.

Service Models

Cloud Software as a Service (SaaS). The capability provided to the consumer is to use the provider's applications running on a cloud infrastructure. The applications are accessible from various client devices through a thin client interface such as a Web browser (e.g., Web-based e-mail). The consumer does not manage or control the underlying cloud infrastructure including network, servers, operating systems, storage, or even individual application capabilities, with the possible exception of limited user-specific application configuration settings.

Cloud Platform as a Service (PaaS). The capability provided to the consumer is to deploy onto the cloud infrastructure consumer-created or acquired applications created using programming languages and tools supported by the provider. The consumer does not manage or control the underlying cloud infrastructure including network, servers, operating systems, or storage, but has control over the deployed applications and possibly application hosting environment configurations.

Cloud Infrastructure as a Service (IaaS). The capability provided to the consumer is to provision processing, storage, networks, and other fundamental computing resources where the consumer is able to deploy and run arbitrary software, which can include operating systems and applications. The consumer does not manage or control the underlying cloud infrastructure but has control over operating systems, storage, deployed applications, and possibly limited control of select networking components (e.g., host firewalls).

Deployment Models

Private cloud. The cloud infrastructure is operated solely for an organization. It may be managed by the organization or a third party and may exist on premise or off premise.

Community cloud. The cloud infrastructure is shared by several organizations and supports a specific community that has shared concerns (e.g., mission, security requirements, policy, and compliance considerations). It may be managed by the organizations or a third party and may exist on premise or off premise.

Public cloud. The cloud infrastructure is made available to the general public or a large industry group and is owned by an organization selling cloud services.

Hybrid cloud. The cloud infrastructure is a composition of two or more clouds (private, community, or public) that remain unique entities but are bound together by standardized or proprietary technology that enables data and application portability (e.g., cloud bursting for load-balancing between clouds).

Note: Cloud software takes full advantage of the cloud paradigm by being service oriented with a focus on statelessness, low coupling, modularity, and semantic interoperability.

INFORMATIONWEEK ANALYTICS, JUNE 2009

The major factors when weighing risks are the criticality of the business processes that might be affected by the technology, the sensitivity of the data being moved or accessed, cost, the visibility you have into the provider's controls and your organization's risk appetite.

Simply put, when it comes to integrating a cloud-based technology, the higher the criticality of the business process, the greater the sensitivity of the data involved, and the less

---

Excerpted from *Navigating the Storm: Governance, Risk and Compliance in the Cloud* by Greg Shipley, chief technology officer for Chicago-based information security consultancy Neohapsis.

visibility and due diligence you performed when investigating the provider, the greater the chance of introducing higher levels of risk into your organization. Inversely, the less critical the process, the less sensitive the data, the less risk you'll potentially inherit.

There is of course a distinct difference between potential risk and actual risk, and the two should not be confused. The key to the process isn't saying "no" all the time, but rather, achieving visibility into potential risks and assuring they are in line with your organization's risk appetite. Put another way, it's about going into a relationship with your eyes wide open and ensuring you'll be in a position to manage any newly introduced, cloud-based risks.

Say you're thinking about building a non-mission critical application, perhaps a tool for the marketing team, using a PaaS (platform as a service) offering. The app won't touch any sensitive data, and you've done enough investigation of the provider to know its controls are within your risk-tolerance levels. On the opposite end of the spectrum would be embracing a cloud-based offering that involves data such as personally identifiable information (PII), credit card numbers or any type of highly confidential data while doing little more than asking the provider some questions beforehand. In this scenario, you're rolling the dice. There's potentially a huge amount of risk to be inherited due to the nature of the data, but without adequate visibility, you simply don't know what you're dealing with.

Most real-world scenarios will fall somewhere in between these two examples, but the approach of measuring visibility against criticality is key. There will, of course, be new threats that will creep up over time, but today we believe the top risks associated with cloud computing can be organized into two high-level areas: Operational risk considerations include security, performance, and availability. Business viability and legal and compliance risks comprise the other major area of concern.

We'd argue that 70 to 80 percent of cloud computing risks are no different from the standard third-party outsourcing risks we've been tackling for years. There are, however, a few unique angles that will keep us on our toes. Some items we'll be keeping our eyes on:

- Provider "chaining." The potential for cascading failures increases as cloud providers construct technologies and services on top of other cloud providers. . . .

- Stealth PaaS: Building a new product or service on top of a PaaS platform has its challenges, but what happens if you aren't even aware that PaaS technology is being used? . . .

- New methods of introducing nasty code: How many people using Amazon's EC2 for OS hosting grabbed a public Amazon EC2 Machine Image (AMI) that simply "looked good"? With OS images able to be uploaded by anyone and widely available in public computing clouds, the threat of someone in your organization downloading an OS template preloaded with malware not only exists, it's likely.

CLOUD COMPUTING'S PORTABILITY GOTCHA: TRANSFER FEES CAN LEAD TO LOCK-IN AS DATA STORES GROW

There were a couple of "aha" moments for me at the Interop conference's Enterprise Cloud Summit this month. The first was that some companies are already storing hundreds of terabytes of data in the cloud. The second was that it can be a slow and expensive process to move that data from one service provider to another.

By John Foley, *Information Week*, November 28, 2009, 12:00 a.m. (from the November 30, 2009, issue).

The subjects came up in a panel on cloud interoperability, where the discussion shifted from APIs to cloud brokers to emerging standards. The panelists were Jason Hoffman, founder and CTO of Joyent; Chris Brown, VP of engineering with Opscode; consultant John Willis of Zabovo; and Bitcurrent analyst Alistair Croll. The gist was that we're still in the early days when it comes to cloud interoperability and that while Amazon's API may be the center of the cloud universe right now, it's hardly enough.

The discussion turned to portability, the ability to move data and applications from one cloud environment to another. There are many reasons IT organizations might do that: dissatisfaction with a cloud service provider, new and better alternatives, and a change in strategy, to name a few. The issue hit home earlier this year when cloud startup Coghead shut down and SAP took over only its assets and engineering team, forcing customers to find a new home for the applications that had been hosted there.

The bigger the data store, the harder the job of moving from one cloud to another. Some companies are putting hundreds of terabytes of data—even a petabyte—into the cloud, according to panel members, and some of these monster databases are reportedly in Amazon's Simple Storage Service. Amazon's S3 price list gives a discount for data stores over 500 TB, so that's entirely feasible.

"Customers with hundreds of terabytes in the cloud: You are no longer portable, and you're not going to be portable, so get over it," Joyent CTO Hoffman said.

It can take weeks or months to move a petabyte of data from one cloud to another, depending on data transfer speeds, Hoffman said. And Amazon charges 10 cents per gigabyte to transfer data out of S3, which comes to $100,000 per petabyte. (That's after you've already spent $100,000 or more in transfer fees moving the data into S3.)

Amazon estimates it would take one to two days to import or export 5 TB of data over a 100-Mbps connection. It has in beta testing a work-around called AWS Import/Export that lets customers load or remove data using portable storage devices, bypassing the network. Amazon recommends that approach if loading data would take a week or more.

What's the lesson? Getting started in the cloud may be fast, cheap, and easy, but the longer you're there, the harder it is to move. As data accumulates, IT needs to monitor not just what it's spending on cloud storage, but also how big the tab to get out is. Price out an exit plan.

GLOSSARY

Amazon EC2: The Elastic Compute Cloud, or computing infrastructure as a service over the Internet, supplied by the Amazon Web Services unit of Amazon.com. Customers rent time on a virtual server running in EC2.

Cache memory: Part of the server's random access memory that is set aside to serve the needs of running applications. It holds frequently used data or parts of applications that are needed to complete a job. The use of cache memory speeds operations and is often employed as a resource combined from multiple servers in cloud computing techniques.

Cloud app: An application designed to be run in the cloud or already installed in the cloud for use by customers.

Cloudburst: A burst or spike of data center activity that is offloaded to a cloud facility for processing, easing the strain on the data center. An earlier meaning sometimes applies: a breach of the cloud, or a customer's inability to reach his own data.

Cloud envy: The tendency of vendors to rename something in their product to include the term *cloud*, without necessarily reengineering any part of the product. See *cloudwashing*.

Cloud lock-in: A level of difficulty, often arbitrarily imposed by a vendor, in moving a workload from one cloud supplier to another. Small differences in virtual machine file formats are one current form of lock-in.

Cloud portability: The ability to move workloads from one cloud vendor to another without the need to execute a file format conversion.

Cloud provider: A supplier of cloud services—hardware servers, software, storage, or all three—from a data center on the Internet.

Cloud storage: A cloud's offering of a disk storage service. Some clouds, such as Amazon's Simple Storage Service (S3), offer storage as part of their infrastructure; others, such as Nirvanix, make storage their primary service.

Cloudwashing: When a vendor adds the word *cloud* to the name of a product or service that used to go by another name.

Column-oriented database: A database that stores data in the columns of a table. The dominant form of relational database uses rows. The column technique allows large numbers of similar items to be aggregated and evaluated quickly. Examples are Sybase IQ and Vertica.

Complex event processing: The ability to define specific events taking place in the software infrastructure, such as a transaction, with the intent of establishing norms, detecting deviations, and setting parameters around acceptable event sequences. Events may be queried for frequency of occurrence in specific time frames.

Elastic Block Store: An Amazon Web Services service on the Elastic Compute Cloud (EC2). It provides temporary storage for an application and its data as the application is running.

Elasticity: The ability of a computing resource to expand and contract as needed; a function of workload balancing and application performance management in the multitenant cloud. When needed, additional virtual machines are brought online.

Eucalyptus: An open source project that duplicated the basic Web service application programming interfaces (APIs) of the Amazon Elastic Compute Cloud (EC2). It supplies an interface equivalent to the ones that load a virtual machine into the EC2 engine or invoke Amazon Simple Storage Service (S3).

Eucalyptus Systems: The company formed by Rich Wolski, Woody Rollins, and others to build commercial products out of Eucalyptus open source code.

External cloud: Usually a cloud service that is available to the public over the Internet, such as Rackspace Cloud, GoGrid, or Amazon Elastic Compute Cloud (EC2).

Firewall: An appliance sitting at the perimeter of the corporation inspecting network traffic for malware, such as Trojans, worms, and viruses, or inappropriate coding instructions inserted where they do not belong.

Framework: An application development platform that provides much of the plumbing to connect the newly developed business logic in an application to the network, databases, application server middleware, and the Web server.

FTP: File Transfer Protocol, the first protocol for moving files from one Internet Protocol (IP) address to another.

Google App Engine: A Google-sponsored cloud infrastructure that supplies more automated administrative support for running applications. It is limited, however, to running applications composed in Python or Java or in a language designed to run in the Java Virtual Machine, such as JRuby or Groovy.

Hadoop: An Apache Software open source project that uses parallel processing in the cloud to retrieve and analyze large amounts of data. Yahoo! is a leader in the project and uses Hadoop to analyze the contents of the World Wide Web on clusters of 4,000 servers.

HTTP: Hypertext Transfer Protocol, the specified networking software that underlies the movement of Web pages and other data over the Internet.

Hypervisor: A layer of virtualization software, also known as a virtual machine manager, that apportions a host server's resources among multiple virtual machines, passing their requests for services to the hardware. The hypervisor handles all communications between applications and the hardware.

Infrastructure as a service (IaaS): One of the major forms of cloud computing. An online service, such as Amazon Web Services Elastic Cloud Compute (EC2), provides raw compute power on a per hour basis.

Internet: The worldwide network that grew out of the DARPA project to establish a communications network that could suffer a failure at any given point and continue to function. It's based on the Transmission Control Protocol/Internet Protocol (TCP/IP), which can route around a point of failure.

Loosely coupled: A method of computing over a shared network where two systems don't need to know very much about each other in order to exchange vital information.

Mainframe: A large, general-purpose computer; the first was the IBM 360 in 1964, and a succession of generations has followed, including the zSeries from IBM that is available today.

Maintenance: In data center operations, the effort required to maintain the production systems necessary to the business and keep them running smoothly. Maintenance tends to take up three-quarters of the typical information technology department budget. New initiatives vie for resources with maintenance.

MapReduce: A combined software function, running on a large server cluster, that pulls data off a set of disks simultaneously, maps it to the cluster processor that is closest to it in 64- or 128-megabyte chunks, then "reduces" or performs a sorting or filtering process on the data. MapReduce, for example, can determine how many times a keyword occurs in the chunk, a function of search. The function originated at Google and is used by Amazon and Yahoo!.

Master/slave: A situation in which a client machine (the slave) is tied to a large server (the master). No matter how intelligent the client may be, it is never called upon to think for itself. It does only what the master tells it to. Mainframes sending displays to dumb terminals is the classic master/slave relationship; large servers on the Internet sending Hypertext Markup Language (HTML) pages to the browser window on a PC is another.

Multitenant: The use of a server in a cloud to provide computer services to more than one customer. Also, the use of an application in the cloud to provide services to more than one customer, such as Salesforce.com customer relationship management (CRM). A multitenant application needs a greater ability to scale up for many users than the standard business application.

Open source code: A method of developing code through a collaborative, voluntary group process in which the resulting application or piece of software is made freely available through download over the Internet.

Peer to peer: A pattern of computing in which two computers interact, and the intelligence at each end of the interaction comes fully into play without one assuming dominance over the other. The opposite of master/slave computing.

Perl: A scripting language designed to manage servers and used by system administrators; often invoked to tie together diverse elements on a Web site.

PHP: Formerly Personal Home Page, a language for hobbyists building Web pages. PHP was recomposed by Andi Gutmans and Zeev Suraski into PHP 3.0 for professional Web site builders. It is a dynamic language that runs the latest changes made in a program without needing to be compiled. It's used to link a database to a Web application, for example. It is open source code and is sometimes referred to as the P in the open source LAMP stack.

Platform as a service: A cloud platform, such as Salesforce .com's Visualforce and Apex, where an application can be developed that conforms to the platform's application pattern and can be run in a cloud that supports the platform, such as Force.com.

Private cloud: The portion of the enterprise data center that can be organized around cloud principles, usually a cluster of x86 servers that are accessible to private company employees and business partners, who can self-provision virtual machines. A goal of building a private cloud is often to coordinate activities with a public cloud. Also known as an internal cloud.

Public cloud: A data server where compute resources are made available to any member of the public who is willing to pay for them; Amazon Elastic Cloud Compute (EC2), Microsoft Azure, and Google App Engine are all examples.

Python: A popular Web site scripting or dynamic language, like PHP and Perl.

Relational database: A data storage system based on a relational model built from mathematical set theory. The relational model relies on tables composed of columns and rows and was composed by IBM researcher Edgar Codd.

REST: Representational State Transfer, or a high-performance, lightweight method of conducting exchanges between two systems over the Internet using only XML for tagging data and SOAP for transferring it.

Ruby on Rails: A dynamic language (Ruby) developed in Japan that was given a framework aiding the fast development of applications. The Rails framework handles some programming conventions, connections, and application programming interface (API) manipulations automatically.

S3: Simple Storage Service, a permanent storage service in the cloud at Amazon's Web Services' Elastic Compute Cloud (EC2). It can be invoked through simple Web Service interfaces and stores data as objects, which can be retrieved through a unique key that S3 assigns them.

Simple API for Cloud Application Services: An open source project led by Zend Technologies to produce application programming interfaces for particular cloud services. Applications using a Simple API could access each service provider that has adopted that particular interface, giving the application cross-cloud capabilities.

SimpleDB: A database service available at Amazon Web Services Elastic Compute Cloud that can store and query data without the administrative overhead of a relational database system. It can deal with large data sets sent to be processed on a cluster of servers.

SOA: Services-oriented architecture, or a way of organizing enterprise applications as a set of independent services. SOA concepts led to the establishment of clear Web services standards that enable many exchanges in cloud computing.

SOAP: Simple Object Access Protocol, a standard way to send eXtensible Markup Language (XML) documents and other files over the Web, with instructions included on what is to be done with the content once it arrives.

Software as a service (SaaS): A form of cloud computing that makes applications available from an online data center. Many users make use of the application at the same time, driving economies of scale. Salesforce.com is a pioneer of SaaS.

Spike: A jump in traffic to a Web server or a demand by a running application for a sudden increase in processor cycles.

TCP/IP: Transmission Control Protocol/Internet Protocol, a resilient networking protocol on which the Internet is based; it automatically routes around switch or router outages.

Virtual appliance: An application along with its operating system, usually optimized to work together, packaged as a virtual machine and able to be moved over the network as a single file. Virtual appliances are often built to run in a target public cloud facility, such as an Amazon Machine Image for Elastic Compute Cloud (EC2). Upon receipt, a public cloud can automatically load and run the virtual appliance.

Virtual machine: A unit of a physical server that has been divided into multiple virtual servers, controlled by software. Each owns a share of the CPU and other physical resources and is supervised by a shared hypervisor, which manages calls for hardware services and resolves conflicts.

Workload: A common data center term for an application and the data it must process in a discrete job on a server. In cloud computing, workloads tend to be formatted as virtual appliances (which include an operating system and other components) and sent to a cloud, where they are run.

WSDL: Web Services Description Language, a standard way of describing services available over the Internet.

Xen: An open source hypervisor that has been adopted and modified for use as the governing hypervisor in the Amazon Web Services Elastic Compute Cloud (EC2). Xen is also the basis of virtualization products from the XenSource unit of Citrix Systems and from Oracle and Sun.

XML: eXtensible Markup Language, a subset of General Markup Language, used in building SOAP-based Web services on the Internet. XML governs the content of a Web page.

INDEX

ABOUT THE AUTHOR

Charles Babcock is one of three editor-at-large writers at *Informa-tionWeek* and its online publication, www.informationweek.com, a United Business Media publication, reporting on the technology industry and business concerns of the IT manager. He has been with the magazine for seven years. He is charged with reporting on virtualization, databases, emerging integration technologies, and new Web technologies. Babcock is the former New York correspondent, software editor, and technical editor of *Computerworld*. He is a former technology editor of *Interactive Week* and former editor in chief of *Digital News*. He is a graduate of Syracuse University with a BS degree in journalism. He is co-winner of the Jesse H. Neal business award for a July 2003 *Baseline* magazine cover story, "McBust," on a failed effort to revamp computing systems at McDonald's Corp. He lives in San Francisco with his wife, Kathleen.

InformationWeek was founded in 1979 and is a leading business technology media brand, delivering practical and thought-provoking analysis on IT issues and trends. *InformationWeek* reaches more than 2 million unique Web site users, 440,000 magazine subscribers, and thousands of analyst report readers and conference attendees. It helps IT managers frame and define their business technology objectives and make IT purchasing decisions.

Cutting-Edge Virtualization Guides

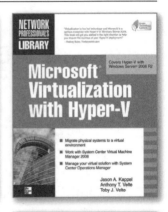